StandFor Digital

Dear Student,

The code below gives you access to the user's area at the **StandFor Digital website**. There, you'll find a variety of multimedia content to make your learning experience more interactive.

Register at **digital.standfor.com.br** and activate the code to start using all the resources that accompany your course book. You can also download your interactive digital book.

1158.4561.GHPP.LJE7.TJ2

With **StandFor Digital** all the resources you need are just a click away!

19998278

Susan Banman Sileci
Patrick Jackson

LIKE US

STUDENT BOOK

1

StandFor

StandFor

© 2017 – StandFor

Editorial Director Lauri Cericato
Editorial Manager Cayube Galas
Editorial Coordinator Ana Carolina Costa Lopes
Assistant Editor Renata Chimim
Content Editor Magueda Lopes Souza
Editorial Assistant Nathalia Xavier Thomaz
Contributors Camila Marques, Maria Luciana Gomes, Mariana Ricardo de Carvalho Ranzeiro, Mauricio Shiroma
Editorial Trainee Fernanda Valezini Ferreira
Linguistic Advisor Edward Willson
Production Manager Mariana Milani
Production Coordinator Marcelo Henrique Ferreira Fontes
Proofreading and Copyediting Coordinator Lilian Semenichin
Proofreading and Copyediting Supervisor Beatriz Carneiro
Copy Editors Amanda di Santis, Claudia Anazawa, Iraci Miyuki Kishi
Proofreaders Enymilia Guimarães, Marcella Arruda, Tatiana Jaworski
Art Manager Ricardo Borges
Art Coordinator Daniela Di Creddo Máximo
Design Sergio Cândido
Cover Design Sergio Cândido
Art Supervisor Patrícia De Michelis
Art Editors Anderson Sunakozawa, Lidiani Minoda
Layout Casa de Ideias
Digital Image Processing Technicians Ana Isabela Pithan Maraschin, Eziquiel Racheti
Illustrations and Cartography Coordinator Marcia Berne
Illustrations Alexandre Dubiela, Aline Sentone, Casa de Ideias, Chris Borges, Eduardo Medeiros, Evertoons, Fabio Eugenio, Galvão Bertazzi, Itamar Dutra, Ivan Coutinho, Kris Zullo, Leandro Lassmar, NiD POSSIBILIDADES ILUSTRADAS, Tel Coelho/Giz de Cera
Photo Researcher Supervisor Elaine Cristina Bueno
Photo Researchers Rosa Andre, Erika Neves do Nascimento
Operations Director and Print Production Manager Reginaldo Soares Damasceno

Dados Internacionais de Catalogação na Publicação (CIP)
(Câmara Brasileira do Livro, SP, Brasil)

Sileci, Susan Banman
Like us : volume 1 / Susan Banman Sileci, Patrick Jackson. – 1. ed. – São Paulo : FTD, 2017.
ISBN 978-85-96-01012-2 (aluno)
ISBN 978-85-96-01013-9 (professor)
1. Inglês (Ensino fundamental) I. Jackson, Patrick. II. Título.

17-03019 CDD-372.652

Índices para catálogo sistemático:
1. Inglês : Ensino fundamental 372.652

The publisher would like to thank the following for permission to reproduce the photographs:

2 3 4 5 6 7 8 9

Em respeito ao meio ambiente, as folhas deste livro foram produzidas com fibras obtidas de árvores de florestas plantadas, com origem certificada.

AFLO/ZUMAPRESS.com/Easypix Brasil: p. **63** (transparent house) Rodrigo Reyes Maran. **AFP:** pp. **13** (Sebastião Salgado) YASUYOSHI CHIBA; **19** (Ben Southall) Torsten Blackwood; **60** (kitchen) Roques Rogery; **62** (Soccer Ball House) Koichi Kamoshida; **79** (children) A.H.M. Rezman; **119** (Angelina and Brad Pitt family) Toru Yamanaka. **AFP/Getty Images:** p. **63** (car house) Franz Neumayr. **AP Photo/Glow Images:** p. **51** (laser keyboard) imagine china; **Alamy/Fotoarena:** p. **85** (domino clock) Olekcii Mach. **Alamy/Glow Images:** pp. **11** (game designer) Jens Kalaene; **15** (meteorologist) Rosalrene Betancourt 7; (geologists) Jeff Morgan 13; **28** (William I) Photo Researchers, Inc.; **29** (Camilla) Andrew Lloyd; (Princess Diana) Allstar Picture Library; **36** (computer) YAY Media AS; **37** (picture) George Mdivanian; **37-3** (old camera) icona; **37-4** (Polaroid camera) Felix Choo; **38** (old computer & old computer advertisement) The Advertising Archives; **39** (old video game) Justin Towell; **56** (bedroom) Patti McConville; **67** (frisbee) Henry Westheim; **78** (Bangladesh girl) Angela Bellas; **79** (Bangladesh girl) Images&Stories; **85** (mistery clock) Classic Image; **113** (cake decorator) Kzenon. **Alamy/Latinstock:** p. **33** (ID Card) Dinodia Photos. **AP Photo /Glow Images:** pp. **17** (baby tiger) Tim Brakemeier; **Barcoft Media/Getty Images:** p. **14** (zoologist) ZSL London Zoo; **Barcoft Media/Other Images:** p. **40** (Lisa Courtney) John Robertson; **Corbis/Glow Images:** p. **77** (children) Randy Faris. **Contributor/Getty Images:** p. **85** (water clock) Universal Images Group **Easypix:** pp. **89** (Jamie Oliver) Andy Butterton; **127** (Audrey Hepburn) Album Cinema. **Easypix Brasil:** pp. **127** (Crease) Everett; **142** (girls eating noodles) Frank Siteman. **EyeEm/Getty Images:** pp. **36** (bird) Joseph Varela; **50** (headphone) Boér Koppány. **FilmMagic/Getty Images:** p. **119** (Jay-Z and Beyonce) Jason LaVeris; **127** (spider man & superman) Everett. **Fotoarena:** pp. **84** (blue water clock) Carlos Eduardo de Quadros; (plant oclock) Alexandre Carvalho; **127** (noodle) Bridgeman. **G.Pestalozzi:** p. **13** (Gabriela Kapim). **Gamma-Rapho/Getty Images:** p. **69** (video game) Gilles Bassignac. **Getty Images:** pp. **25** (Migrant Mother) Science Source; **35** (digital phone) Yagi Studio; **37 - 1** (old camera) SSPL; **60** (floating house) RubberBall Productions; **71** (teenagers) mixetto; **77** (kids in school) kali9; **83** (girl) RichLegg; **98** (Beckham family) Jeff Vespa; **127** (Nick Minaj) Kevin Mazur; (Neymar) Laurence Griffiths; **134** (boy yawning) China Photos. **GETTY IMAGES ASIAPAC/Getty Images/AFP:** p. **62** (Soccer Ball house) Koichi Kamoshida. **Glow Images:** pp. **15** (man with telescope) Erik Isakson; **40** (child with stuffed animal & child using computer) John Robertson; **70** (hip-hop) Deposit Photos. **Icon SMI/Getty Images:** p. **73** (X games) Tony Donaldson. **Koreabizwire:** p. **25** (South Korean family) Yonhap. **LightRocket/Getty Images:** p. **79** (classroom) Jonas Gratzer. **Latinstock:** p. **15** (scientist) SPL DC. **Living4Media Editorial/Latinstock:** p. **60** (bedroom) Bouchet, Guy. **London News:** p. **59** (gates) Vickie Flores. **Los Angeles Times/Getty Images:** p. **123** (futuristic bag) Glenn Koenig. **Minden Pictures/Latinstock:** p. **18** (baby panda) Katherine Feng. **ONLY WORLD/Only France/AFP**: p. **60** (kitchen) Roques Rogery. **Picture-alliance/dpa/AP/Glow Images:** p. **17** (zoologist) Tim Brakemeier. **IVORY COAST/REUTERS/Latinstock:** p. **62** (crocodile) Thierry Gouegnon. **REUTERS/Latinstock:** pp. **62** (Airplane house) Aziz Taher; **63** (stone house) Paulo Whitaker. **SCIENCE PHOTO LIBRARY/SPLDC/Latinstock:** p. **15** (biologist) ALEXIS ROSENFELD. **Shutterstock.com:** pp. **6** (speaker) Krisztian; (book) Artizarus; (pencil) iconmama; (reading) browndogstudios; (speaking) Vector; (question mark) Orla; (interrogation) iDesign; **7** (book) MTrebbin; (pen) Pamela D. Maxwell; (whiteboard) Nemida; (chair) Luis Santos; (pencil) Boltenkoff; (boy and girl) Syda Productions; (desk) Michael Courtney; **8** (color pencil) Libor Fousek; **9** (friends at school) Lisa F. Young; **10** (background pictures) Creativa Images; (graphic designer) wavebreakmedia; (tour guide) Milan Gonda; **11** (actor) Nicoleta Ionescu; (cake decorator) Africa Studio; (photographer) Maridav; (singer) s_bukley; (veterinarian) eurobanks; (controller) Nata-Lia; (mixer) ProstoSvet; (food) MARCHPN; (draw) inspired_by_the_light; (butterfly) spline_x; (camera) science photo; (dog) Igor Normann; (trophy) MISHELLA; (microphone) Brian A Jackson; (map) Thinglass; (architectural project) Dimitar Sotirov; (boy) TunedIn by Westend61; (monitor) Gorbash Varvara; **12** (Beyonce) Ovidiu Hrubaru; (Zac Efron) DFree; (veterinarians) Tyler Olson; (singer) Stokkete; (photographers) pisaphotography; (chefs) Africa Studio; (graphic design) ESB Professional (tourists) Ken Schulze; **13** (Taylor Swift) Everett Collection; (Jennifer Lawrence) Featureflash Photo Agency; **14** (marine biologist) Abd. Halim Hadi; (astronomer) Ginn Tinn Photography; (botanist) Dragon Images; (meteorologist) Rawpixel.com; (geologist) Paul B. Moore (background moon) Claudio Divizia; **15** (background planet) Romolo Tavani; 15 (agronomist) goodluz; (zoologists) belizar; (telescope) SehrguteFotos; (fishes & coral) Vlad61; (plant) ZaZa Studio; (zebra) Volodymyr Burdiak; (stones) NaughtyNut; (rain) Mr Twister; (tiger) dangdumrong; (sunflower) Vitalii Bashkatov; **17** (kids) Jacek Chabraszewski; (game design) Rawpixel.com; (girl) Tracy Whiteside; **18** (eating chocolate) De Repente; (woman sleeping) Nenad Aksic; **19** (waterslide) Jan Mika; (blond girl) michaeljung; (ginger boy) Jorg Hackemann; (Asian girl) Ronnachai Palas; (African boy) Africa Studio; (boy in brown shirt) Phovoir; **22** (kids) Andi Berger; **23** (middle age man) Phovoir; (middle age woman) Jeanette Dietl; (man smiling) goodluz; (woman smiling) Yuri Shevtsov; (man with the hat) palomadelosrios; (woman with glasses) goodluz; (boy) Pete Pahham; (girl) Sergey Novikov; (teenager girl) dnaveh; (girl in yellow t-shirt) Gino Santa Maria; (boy in red T-shirt) Gelpi; **24** (background picture) Freedom Studio; (couple hugging) michaeljung; (family) Kzenon; (family in the park) F8 studio; (couple smiling) Monkey Business Images; (Hispanic family) Blend Images; **25** (sculpture) Dmitry Erokhin; **27** (Asian friends) Odua Images; (friends) Andy Dean Photography; **29** (Queen Elizabeth II) Shaun Jeffers; (Prince Charles) Mark William Penny; **30** (singer) Billion Photos; (botanist) WAYHOME studio; (veterinarian) didesign021; (geologist) sanek70974; (architect) goodluz; (tour guide) Jenny Leonard; (girls) Sasa Prudkov; **31** (cake decorator) Sergey Chumakov; (veterinarian) Tyler Olson; (singers) DFP Photographic; **32** (backpack) Brunal; (notebook) chrupka; **33** (wallet) tkemot; (cell phone) Bornfree; (video game) julie deshaies; (tablet) Billion Photos; (keys) Neveshkin Nikolay; (pencil case) IB Photography; (laptop) Peter Kotoff; (wallet and key) CHATCHAI SAWATDIPHAP; (DVD covers) ND700; (laptop) Dutin; (smartphone) yurchello108; **34** (tablets) Adam Radosavljevic; (wallets) patpitchaya; (notebook) MELCHENKO NATALIIA; (wallet) Sergiy1975; (pencil case) Artem Shadrin; (notebooks) gutsulyak; **35** (retinal scan) Ahmet Misirligul; (media screen) Sergey Nivens; (digital) Alhovik; (backpack) Maria Savenko; (ID card) RealVector; (vector) Wildjohny; **36** (old bike) DutchScenery; (new bike) steamroller_blues; (heavy) Ververidis Vasilis; (balloon) Etienne du Plessis; (truck) Rob Wilson; (car) Jarretera; (short pencil & long pencil) Ruslan Ivantsov; (baguette) Olga Nayashkova; (sandwich) Phovoir; (ray) Signature Message; (woman and cat) Tynoclub; (woman) Blend Images; (blackboard) Kutlayev Dmitry; (man carrying books) ESB Essentials; (books) SibFilm; **37-2** (old camera) John Gomez; **37-5** (digital camera) Scanrail1; **39** (kids) SergiyN; (notebook) Valentin Agapov; (smartphone) Leszek Kobusinski; **41** (coin) SNEHIT; (stamp) spatuletail; (rock) Mrs_ya; (clock) Dima Moroz; (cap) Pincarel; (comic) urbanbuzz; (teddy bear) Obak; (badge) Mr Doomits; **42** (T-shirt) Magabi; (sweatshirt) BEAUTYofLIFE; **43** (jeans) elenovsky; (sneakers) MichaelJayBerlin; (jacket) Ruslan Semichev; (skirt) Semen Lixodeev; (dress) Tarzhanova; (cap) Everything; (shirt) indigolotos; (socks) Oleksandr Lybitskiy; **44** (red sweatshirt) sagir; (vintage dress) Tarzhanova; (blue dress) fashionall; **46** (twenty-one) Rafael Croonen; (twenty-two) Ralf Herschbach; (twenty-three) cankuskon; (thirty) kenkistler; (forty) David Lee; (fifty) xfox01; (sixty) cimbat2; (seventy) Sebastian Kaulitzki; (eighty) Bruno Ferrari; (ninety) igorstevanovic; (one hundred) Tony Baggett; (yellow cap) vitaliy_73; (green shoes) Elnur; (jeans) badahos; **47** (food) Iuliia photographer; (jeans) Karkas; (ticket) Ianinas; (sunglasses) exopixel; (video game) Svetislav1944; (cellphone) Umberto Shtanzman; (shoes) bdstudio; (earphone) Dragonskydrive; (dollar) David Franklin; **50** (karaoke machine) ©erics; (USB light) GzP_Design; (drone) Valentin Valkov; **51** (sports kit) Africa Studio; (instruments kit) Zheltyshev; (art kit) matka_Wariatka; – (background houses) romakoma; (living room) ppa; (bedroom) Photographee.eu; **55** (kitchen) Gordon Ball LRPS; (bathroom) Atiketta Sangasaeng; (dining room) Artazum; (yard) Susan Law Cain; (sofa) Ivan Smuk; (TV) rosesmith; (bed) Dima Moroz; (table) Andrew Mayovskyy; (fridge) Ppart; (bookshelf) Who is Danny; **56** (living room) Armando Frazao; (girl using cell phone) eakkaluktemwanich; **57** (girl using tablet) Farknot Architect; **58** (Background castle) Julia700702; (castle) Pecold; (tower) Andrey Starostin; (door & wall) Carlos Caetano; (window) InnaFelker; (knight) Slawomir Fajer; (moat) Aerovista Luchtfotografie; (hall) Bildagentur Zoonar GmbH; (drawbridge) John Panella; (flag) Alfonso de Tomas; **59** (Tower of London) Sergii Rudiuk; (beefeaters) Kiev.Victor; (crows) Red Squirrel; **60** (living room) ostill; (girl) WAYHOME studio; (boy) Age Fotostock; **61** (teenagers) Jacek Chabraszewski; **62** (River House) Tatiana Popova; (Toilet House) BoyCatalyst; **64** (soccer ball & football) Africa Studio (soccer) Mooinblack; (baseball) Aspen Photo; **65** (volleyball) muzsy; (tennis) topten22photo; (basketball) Hin255; (table tennis) Dwphotos; (running) Martin Good; (hitting) Tom Wang; (throwing) Brocreative; (jumping) Dnaveh; (catching) Monkey Business Images; (kicking) Anekoho; (background picture) Arogant; **67-2** (Ultimate team) rSnapshotPhotos; **67-3** (kids playing) Andrew Babble; **67-4** (throwing the Frisbee) Dariush M; **68** (salad) Julian Valentin; (exercising) Kyle Lee; (sleeping) Anton Watman; (drinking water) Paulaphoto; (washing hands) Picturepartners; (having fun) VP Photo Studio; **69-1** (exercise) Lapina; **69-2** (wash the face) Vichni; **69-3** (drink water) Trifonov Igor; **69-5** (sleep) Andrey_Popov; **69-6** (eat good food) Dmytro Vietrov; **70-1** (hip-hop) Lucky Business; (yoga) Oneinchpunch; (football) tammykayphoto; (basketball) Dotshock; **70-2** (football game) Aspen Photo; (basketball game) Eliz60; (yoga class) Rawpixel.com; **71** (Indian girl) Natalia Yankelevich; (basketball) Aspen Photo; **72** (bungee jump) Elina; (paraglider) Kamilpetran; (dive) Sergey Zavgorodny; (surf) EpicStockMedia; (mountain biking) Oleksiy Rezin; (rally) Sportpoint; (snowboarding 1) Ipatov; (skiing) IM_photo; (climb) Photobac; (caverman) Largueitudoefui; **73** (background picture) Parvel Burchenco; (Ashley Fiolek) Warren Price Photography; (Shaun White) Ervin Monn; (Fabiola da Silva) Travis Rowan; (background) Tacio Philip Sansonovski; **75** (brothers) Dmitry Naumov; **76** (get up) Annop Itsarayoungyuen; (breakfast) multiart; **77** (come home) Eileny; (studying) Catalin Petolea; (eat dinner) Monkey Business Images; (shower) VaLiza; (sleep) Patrizia Tilly; **77-3/2** (study) Espies; **77-3/3** (shower) Kamira **77-3/4** (eat lunch) Monkey Business Images; 77-3/5 (boy with backpack) sebra; **79** (boat) simona2016; (library) Sean Pavone; (flood) SIHASAKPRACHUM; **80** (digital clocks) Maxfromhell; (breakfast) Tatyana Vyc; (boy) Rob Marmion; (boy studying) Sergey Novikov; (children eating) anetta; **81** (theater) Ungvari Attila; (theater managers) goodluz; (directors) Claudia K; (orchestra) Pavel L Photo and Video; **83** (boy and girl) Lisa F. Young; **84** (sundial) pr2is; (hourglass) Andrey Burmakin; (background picture) Sparkus design; (blue clock) Sova_31; **85** (Grand Central Station) sarahnev; (Big Ben) Mapics; (The Prague Astronomical Clock) Anastasios71; (boy) Zurijeta; **86** (bread) mama_mia; (pasta) carpe89; **87** (ice cream) stockcreations; (rice) rlat; (eggs) HandmadePictures; (steak) Gregory Gerber; beans) diogoppr; (fish) horvathta (chicken) unpict; **87-4/1** (steak) MaraZe; **87-4/2** (lasagna) stockcreations; **87-4/3** (ice cream) Yeko Photo Studio; **87-4/4** (bread) Monticello; **87-4/5** (egg) Nattika **88** (Jamie Oliver) Featureflash Photo Agency; **89** (boy) Valua Vitaly; **90** (fish and chips) margouillat photo; (noodles) vitals; (tacos) Joshua Resnick; (hamburgers) GooDween123; (sushi) Angeleno; (pizza) Michail Patakos; **91** (tacos) Foodio; (pizza) Africa Studio; (sushi) YuliiaHolovchenko; (hamburger) Valentyn Volkov; (fish and chips) Kelvin Wong; (noodles) fuumi901; (curry) Africa Studio; (fish) neil langan; **92** (server) michaeljung; **93 (friends) Blend Images** (boy) p_ponomareva (presentation) Monkey Business Images; **94** (sugar) Coprid; (cocoa) Happy Stock Photo; (flour) M. Unal Ozmen; (fermento) Kaspri; (salt) artproem; (egg) Nattika (water) anaken2012; (margarine) Eivaisla; (vanilla) Maren Winter; (chocolate cake) Africa Studio; (chocolate brownie) Natalya Arzamasova; (mixing) Tomophafan (background brownie) Anna Shepulova; **95** (temperature) Albert Nowicki; (mould) ffolas; (flour) David Herraez Calzada; (mixing) Oliver Wilde; (brownie dough) Darkkong; (brownies) Andrei Tudoran; (boy eating) gosphotodesign; (background brownie 1) Kim Reinick; (background brownie 2) etorres; **98** (background picture) nav; **100** (background picture) Rasdi Abdul Rahman; (house pool) Ramone; (building) Wondervisuals; (modern house) alexandre zveiger; (sea house); (girl) pinkomelet; **101** (blueprint) Bardocz Peter; (3D project) Photobank gallery; Mike J Roberts; **102** (man) kurhan; (professionals) sheff; **104** (furnitures icons) Iconic Bestiary; (volleyball player) Val Thoermer; **105** (food icon) bioraven; **110** (cake) Oleksandr Chub; (door) sevi gadea; (fish) Brilliance stock; (ice cream) Designsstock (pasta) Billion Photos; (beef) MaraZe; (window) vipman; **112** (couple) Sergey Nivens; (actor) Igor Bulgarin; (veterinarian) Alexander Raths; (graphic designer) scyther5; (photographer) aaltair; (game designer) Rawpixel.com; (nutritionist) PR Image Factory; (singer) Sarah Marchant; (cake decorator) Africa Studio; (tourist guide) Monkey Business Images; **113** (graphic designer) Kaspars Grinvalds; (singers) Nejron Photo; (photographer) Syda Productions; (architect) goodluz (veterinarians) NEstudio; **114** (panda) Hung Chung Chih; (fish) ehtesham; (flower) Nico Muller Art; (sky) Olegusk; (star) RealCG Animation Studio; (rock) Igor Plotnikov; **118** (teenager boy) Anna Omelchenko; (older woman & woman) kurhan; (man) valtrifon; (girl) SergiyN; (older man) Minerva Studio; (boy) Catalin Petolea; **120** (teenager) sixdays24; (ID Card) eteimaging; (video game) TrAj43; (tablet) Liashko; (suitcase) GMEVIPHOTO; (laptop) guteksk7; (keys) remik44992 **121** (iPhone) Leszek Kobusinski; (notebooks) krichie; (ID card) eteimaging; (keys) Gavran333; (video game) Svetislav1944; (laptop) DnD-Production.com; (wallet) tkemot; **122** (mansion) Shelli Jensen; (cake) Irina Suglobova; (red cake) Scruggelgreen; (smartphone) A. Aleksandravicius; (measuttape) Marko Poplasen; (feather) Sarah2; (small house) Susan Law Cain; (metal tape) Arts Vector; (book) Alekseyliss; (weight) Laborant; **122** (books) Peter Baxter; (backpack) Laboko; (sling backpack) Venus Angel; (shoulder bag) Africa Studio; (big backpack) My Good Images; **126** (numbers) iunewind; **127** (girl smiling) sanneberg; (basketball) Natursports; (masculine model) Dorota Zietek; (feminine model) Valua Vitaly; **129** (trailer) MaxPhoto; (couple) Lisa F. Young; (trailer on the road) Tupungato; **131-1** (tree house) suparat chanyoot; **131-2** (red tree house) Lunar Storms; **131-3** (big tree house) Ruta Production; **131-4** (tree house bedroom) Tr1sha; **132** (tennis racket) Billion Photos; (net) GraphicsRF; (ball) Africa Studio; (glove) Scott L. Williams; (basketball) gomolach; 133 (girl & boy) Sergey Novikov; (friends) Monkey Business Images; **134** (ginger girl) Firma V; (earful) Zdravinjo; (food) Eivaisla; (football player) Islandwave; (mother and son) Zdravinjo; **135** (boys with medal & soccer) Muzsy; (basketball & voleyball) Sergey Novikov; (baseball) mTaira; (girls) Syda Productions; (background house) Ievan Georgiev; **136** (morning) artcasta (afternoon) Sumalee; (evening) Vladimir Arndt; (night) Volha Vasilevich; **137** (girl) Monkey Business; (boys) Blend Images; **138** (clock) rem 118; (digital clock) Maxfromhell; **141** (boy) Monkey Business Images; (oriental girl) I love photo; (girl) Hogan Imaging; (blond boy) Valentina Razumova; (bread) Gamzova Olga (chicken) dampuen; (egg) Marian Weyo; (fish) Viktory Panchenko; (ice cream) Dusan Zidar; (pasta) Francesco83; (rice and beans) Vanessa Volk; (salad) Mateus Gzik; (steak) Gregory Gerber; **142** (girl eating sushi) Alexander Trinitatov; (boy eating pizza) Kiselev Andrey Valerevich; (boy eating tacos) 3445128471; (girl eating pasta) Monkey Business Images; (boy eating hamburger) BravissimoS; **143** (hamburger) koss13; (sandwich) Timolina; (ethnic food) Romaset; (tacos) stockcreations. **SPL/LatinStock:** p. **37** (PBill camera) Cordelia Molloy. **SSPL/Easypix:** p. **84** (candle clock) SM. **STAR MAX/IPx/AP/Glow Images:** p. **29** (Prince William) KGC-375; **Stringer/Getty Images:** p. **81** (audience) Peter Bischoff. **Tetra Images/Glow Images:** p. **15** (astronomers) Erik Isakson. **Toronto Star/Getty Images:** p. **38** (old cell phone) John Mahler. **UIG/Getty Images:** p.**11** (nutritionist) BSIP. **WireImage/Getty Images:** p **31** (Prince Andrew) Samir Hussein **98** (David and Victoria) Karwai Tang; **99** (Will Smith family) Jim Spellman. **WireImage for Chase/Getty Images:** p. (Buddy Valastro) John W. Ferguson.

The credits that are not mentioned here have been printed on the page where the artwork appeared due to contract demands.

Todos os direitos reservados à
Editora FTD
Rua Rui Barbosa, 156 – Bela Vista – São Paulo-SP
CEP 01326-010 – Fone 0800-772-2300
Caixa Postal 65149 – CEP da Caixa Postal 01390-970
contato@standfor.com.br – www.standfor.com.br

Produção gráfica
FTD EDUCAÇÃO | GRÁFICA & LOGÍSTICA
Avenida Antônio Bardella, 300 - 07220-020 GUARULHOS (SP)
Fone: (11) 3545-8600 e Fax: (11) 2412-5375

A comunicação impressa e o papel têm uma ótima história ambiental para contar
TWO SIDES
www.twosides.org.br

A - 584.881/19

WELCOME TO LIKE US

Aprender um novo idioma é sempre uma experiência emocionante. Ao aprender inglês, você poderá se conectar e se comunicar com o mundo todo de uma maneira real e transformadora. Isso abrirá um leque de oportunidades e de grandes experiências para você.

LIKE US foi desenvolvido para ser divertido e, sobretudo, para ajudá-lo a aprender o máximo e da melhor maneira possível. Você aprenderá diversas palavras novas e também sobre vários tópicos de seu interesse. Ao longo de seus estudos com **LIKE US**, você desenvolverá suas habilidades de leitura, escrita e de compreensão oral, além de poder falar inglês.

Neste momento, em todo o mundo, há pessoas se comunicando em inglês. É como se fosse uma grande comunidade, e **LIKE US** o ajudará a fazer parte dela. Esperamos que você se divirta conosco nessa experiência.

Os autores

CONTENTS

STARTER UNIT

CLASSROOM OBJECTS

1. Write.

pencil desk book pen chair board backpack

1. b oard
2. b
3. c
4. d
5. p
6. p
7. b

2. Listen, check, and practice. (2)

CLASSROOM LANGUAGE

3. Write the words under the correct picture. Then listen and practice. (3)

Close your book.
How do you say this in English?
Listen.
Open your book.
Read.
Talk to your classmate.
What does this mean?
Write.

1. 

How do you say this in English?

2. 

3. 

4. 

5. 

6. 

7. 

8. 

THE ALPHABET

4. Listen and practice. 4

A	B	C	D	E	F
G	H	I	J	K	L
M	N	O	P	Q	R
S	T	U	V	W	X
		Y	Z		

5. Talk to a classmate. Spell.

GREETINGS

6. Write the expressions.

Hello.
Good morning.
Good afternoon.
Good evening.
~~Good night.~~
Goodbye.

1

2

3

4

5

6

7. Listen, check, and practice. 5

NUMBERS 1–20

8. Complete the chart. Then listen and check. 6

1	one	11	eleven
2	two	12	______
3	______	13	thirteen
4	four	14	fourteen
5	______	15	______
6	six	16	sixteen
7	______	17	seventeen
8	eight	18	______
9	______	19	nineteen
10	ten	20	______

9. Write the numbers to complete the sequences.

1. one ❖ three ❖ five ❖ seven ❖ ______
2. eighteen ❖ ______ ❖ ______ ❖ nine ❖ six
3. four ❖ ______ ❖ twelve ❖ sixteen ❖ ______
4. ______ ❖ twelve ❖ fourteen ❖ ______ ❖ eighteen
5. twenty ❖ ______ ❖ ______ ❖ eleven ❖ eight
6. three ❖ seven ❖ ______ ❖ fifteen ❖ nineteen

COLORS

10. Write the colors. Then listen and practice. 7

brown
______
______
______
______
______
______
______
______
______
______

DAYS OF THE WEEK

11. Complete the calendar with the days of the week. Then listen and practice. 8

Friday ~~Wednesday~~ Monday
Sunday Tuesday Saturday
Thursday

August						
			Wednesday			
1	2	3	4	5	6	7
8	9	10	11	12	13	14
15	16	17	18	19	20	21
22	23	24	25	26	27	28
29	30	31				

MONTHS

12. Write the numbers 1–12 to put the months in the correct order.

LANGUAGE TIP

Many words in English look like words in your language! Which of the months is similar in your language?

April	4
September	9
December	12
August	8
March	3
January	1
June	6
February	2
October	10
July	7
May	5
November	11

13. Listen, check, and practice. 9

14. Talk to your classmates and fill in the chart.

	NAME	BIRTHDAY MONTH	AGE
	Fernando	January	11
1.	João	september	12
2.	sofia	march	7
3.			

1 COOL JOBS!

VOCABULARY

1. Listen and practice. 10

graphic designer

tour guide

Hello! My name is Gabriel. I'm a (1) ______________.

Hello! I'm Simon. I'm a (2) ______________.

Hi! I'm a (3) ______________. My name is Patrick.

Hello! My name is Sarah. I'm a (4) ______________.

Hello. I'm a (5) ______________. My name is Laura.

Hello. I'm Luiz. I'm a (6) ______________.

Hi! I'm Sam. I'm an (7) ______________.

Hi! I'm Petra. I'm a (8) ______________.

Hello! My name is Amanda. I'm an (9) ______________.

LANGUAGE TIP

We use **a** before consonant sounds (b, c, d, f ...) and we use **an** before vowel sounds (a, e, i, o, u).
a nutritionist
an architect

actor

nutritionist

cake decorator

photographer

architect

game designer

singer

veterinarian

2. Read. Then write the words.

3. Listen and check. 11

4. Match the jobs with the objects.

1. actor
2. veterinarian
3. cake decorator
4. photographer
5. singer
6. tour guide
7. game designer
8. architect
9. graphic designer
10. nutritionist

5. Do a classroom survey. Write the top three jobs that your classmates want to do when they are adults.

WORKBOOK, 112

Editoria de arte

GRAMMAR

LANGUAGE TIP
We usually use the short form when we speak.

1. Look at the conversation. Then read the examples in the *Grammar* box.

BE (AFFIRMATIVE)

SHORT FORM	LONG FORM
I'**m** a singer.	I **am** a singer.
You'**re** an architect.	You **are** an architect.
He'**s** a photographer.	He **is** a photographer.
She'**s** a game designer.	She **is** a game designer.
We'**re** veterinarians.	We **are** veterinarians.
They'**re** nutritionists.	They **are** nutritionists.

2. Complete the sentences with *am*, *are*, or *is*.

1. You ______ an actor.
2. Michael ______ a tour guide.
3. They ______ graphic designers.
4. Will ______ a teacher.
5. I ______ a cake decorator.
6. We ______ nutritionists.

3. Complete the paragraphs with the short form of the verbs.

1. This is Neil. ______ a veterinarian. He works with dogs and cats.

2. This is Gloria. ______ a singer. She sings rock music. She likes pop music too.

3. Xavier and Carolina are from New York. ______ cake decorators. The cake is beautiful!

4. André likes the USA. "______ a tour guide. I live in Chicago, but I love Los Angeles and Seattle too!"

5. "______ photographers," say John and Claire. Emmanuel is their favorite model.

6. This is Isaac. ______ a game designer. He designs sports games, and he loves football.

READING

4. Look at the pictures in **Activity 5**. What magazine is it?

a. Sports and Adventures b. Celebrities! c. Animals

5. Read the magazine article and listen. 12

Buddy Valastro is the "Cake Boss." He's a famous cake decorator. He has a reality TV show, and his cakes are delicious.

Gabriela Kapim is a nutritionist. She has a popular TV show, and she helps kids with nutrition. Gabriela thinks kids have to exercise, too.

This is **Taylor Swift**. She's an American singer, and she is extremely popular. She has sold over 40 million albums!

Jennifer Lawrence is an actor. She starred in interesting movies like *X-Men: First Class* and *The Hunger Games*.

Sebastião Salgado is a famous Brazilian photographer. His pictures are usually in black and white, not color. His most famous pictures are of rural workers in Brazil.

6. Check ✔ the correct column and write two more examples. Then talk to your classmates.

	ACTOR	ARCHITECT	CAKE DECORATOR	GAME DESIGNER	GRAPHIC DESIGNER	NUTRITIONIST	PHOTOGRAPHER	SINGER	TOUR GUIDE	VETERINARIAN
1. BUDDY VALASTRO			✔							
2. GABRIELA KAPIM						✔				
3. TAYLOR SWIFT								✔		
4. JENNIFER LAWRENCE	✔									
5. SEBASTIÃO SALGADO							✔			
6. ______										
7. ______										

WORKBOOK, 113

CLIL SCIENCE

GRAMMAR

1. **Listen and practice. Then read the sentences in the *Grammar* box.** 13

1 marine biologist

4 meteorologist

2 astronomer

5 geologist

3 botanist

6 zoologist

IMPORTANTE

BE (NEGATIVE)

SHORT FORM	LONG FORM
I'**m not** a marine biologist.	I **am not** a marine biologist.
You **aren't** an astronomer.	You **are not** an astronomer.
He **isn't** a botanist.	He **is not** a botanist.
She **isn't** a meteorologist.	She **is not** a meteorologist.
We **aren't** geologists.	We **are not** geologists.
They **aren't** zoologists.	They **are not** zoologists.

C.C

2. **Write negative sentences. Use the short form.**

1. He / botanist — He isn't a botanist.
2. I / meteorologist — I'm not meteorologist
3. You / marine biologist — you're not marine biologist
4. She / astronomer — SHE'S not astronomer
5. They / zoologists — THEY're not zoologists

JOBS IN SCIENCE

3. Listen and complete the sentences. Circle the words that end with *-ist*. 14

C.C

1. She's a marine (biologist). She studies the **ocean**.
2. They're astronomaer. They study the **stars** with a **telescope**.
3. He's a botanist. He studies **plants**.
4. She's a meteurologist. She isn't a marine biologist. She looks at the **weather**.
5. They're geologist. They aren't botanists. Geologists look at **rocks**.
6. They're zoologist. They study **animals**.

4. Look at the pictures. Write the sentences.

C.C

1. He  He's an astronomer. He isn't a marine biologist.
2. She  SHE'S a [illegible] botaniste. SHE'S not a zoologist.
3. They  They're geologist. THEY're not meteurologist.
4. She  SHE'S biologist. SHE'S not geologist.
5. We  We're zoologist. We're not botaniste.

WORKBOOK, 114

COMMUNICATION

1. Look at the pictures in **Activities 2** and **4**. Check ✔ the people you can see.

1. ✔ meteorologist
2. ☐ veterinarian
3. ☐ marine biologist
4. ☐ tour guide
5. ☐ singer
6. ☐ botanist
7. ☐ actor
8. ☐ architect

2. Read.

3. Read **Activity 2** again. Then complete the sentences.

1.  She's a botanist. She's fine.
2.  He's an ______________. He's ______________.
3.  They're ______________. They're ______________.

4. Listen and write *great*, *fine*, or *OK*. 15

5. Listen and practice. 16

LANGUAGE TIP

You can also say:

How's it going?	Not bad.
How are you doing?	I'm OK, thanks.
Hey! What's up?	Nothing much.

17 PRONUNCIATION

Silent /e/ at the end of words.

- game
- fine
- name
- cake

6. Read about Kevin. Then write about Sophia.

Kevin Martin

Sophia Wright

Hi, I'm ...

7. Talk to your classmates.

WORKBOOK, 115

BONUS Magazine

DREAM JOBS!

1. Answer the questions. Then talk with your classmate.

1. What is your dream job?
2. What do the words in the box mean?

water slide	bed	pandas
chocolate	the ocean	

2. Read the list of dream jobs.

PANDA HUGGER

This job is to hug pandas all day long for $32,000 a year.

You have to:

- be over 22 years old
- know about pandas
- have good writing and photography skills

CHOCOLATE TASTER

For this job you must eat five boxes of chocolate a day.

You have to:

- meet suppliers
- check quality
- research the competitors

BED TESTER

This is a good job for sleepy people!

You have to:

- stay all day in bed
- sleep in a bed store
- write about beds

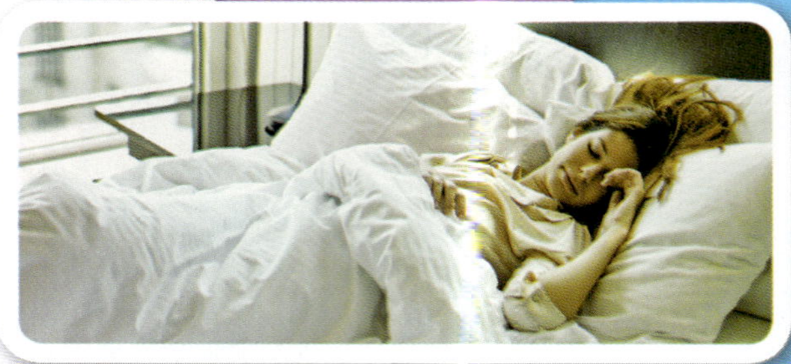

WATERSLIDE TESTER

For this job, you will travel around the world riding waterslides.

You will need:
- courage
- swimming ability
- good writing skills

Editoria de Arte

ISLAND CARETAKER

This job is in the Great Barrier Reef, in Australia. You must go to the beach every day.

You have to:
- swim in the ocean
- write a blog
- make videos and take photos

3. What is the best job for these people? Write the job titles.

I enjoy water parks.

Waterslide Tester

I want to travel and go to the beach.

____

I sleep 12 hours every night.

____

I love animals.

____

I want to eat lots of chocolate.

____

4. How about you? Write 1–5 in the order you would like the jobs.

☐ Bed Tester ☐ Chocolate Taster ☐ Panda Hugger

☐ Island Caretaker ☐ Waterslide Tester

UNIT 2

FAMILY FUN

VOCABULARY

1. Listen, read, and write the words. 18

1. He's my brother. His name is Jesse. He's twelve.
2. She's my sister. Her name is Agatha. She's fourteen.

LANGUAGE TIP

If you don't know, ask, **How do you say ______ in English?**

3. He's my ______. His name is Mark. He's a marine biologist.
4. She's my ______. Her name is Diane. She's a graphic designer.
5. He's my ______. His name is Joseph. He's a veterinarian.
6. She's my ______. Her name is Maxine. She's an architect.
7. He's my ______, George. He's my father's brother. He's a botanist.
8. She's my ______. She's a cake decorator. Her name is Roberta.
9. She's my ______, Natalie. My uncle is her father.

LANGUAGE TIP

People often call their mother **Mom**. Here are some other ways people talk about their family members:
father = **dad**
grandmother = **grandma**
grandfather = **grandpa**

2. Listen and check. 19

3. Read about David and his family. Complete the paragraph with the family words.

David's (1) ______ is an architect. His (2) ______ is George. His (3) ______ is a marine biologist. David's (4) ______ Roberta is a cake decorator. His (5) ______ is Diane. He is Agatha's (6) ______. Agatha is Jesse's (7) ______. David's (8) ______ is a veterinarian. David's (9) ______ is Natalie.

4. Write the names and jobs of some of the people in your family.

Family member	Job

GRAMMAR

LANGUAGE TIP
We write **Who is he?** or **Who's he?** They're the same.

1. Look at the conversation. Then read the examples in the *Grammar* box.

WHO POSSESSIVE ADJECTIVES AND 'S					
WHO IS HE?			**WHO ARE THEY?**		
He's	my your his her our their	father.	They're	my your his her our their	sisters.
Possessive 's He's Michael's father. She's my father's sister.			**Possessive 's** They're Michael's sisters. They're my father's sisters.		

20 PRONUNCIATION
Homophones
We pronounce *they're*, *their*, and *there* the same.

2. Look at the pictures. Then circle the correct option.

1. 
• James – Kylee
James is *my* / *his* / *her* uncle.

2. 
• Maya – Kylee an her brothers
Maya is *his* / *her* / *their* aunt.

3. 
• Bill – Kylee and her brothers
Bill is *your* / *her* / *their* grandfather.

4. 
• Brian – my brothers and I
Brian is *his* / *her* / *our* cousin.

5. 
• Jeremy – Kylee's brother
Jeremy is *my* / *his* / *her* brother.

6. 
• Lola – Jay and Annie
Lola is *my* / *his* / *their* dog.

READING

3. Read and complete the family tree with names and jobs.

This is the Carter family. Alan is Beth's brother. He's 12. His favorite color is blue. Annette is Alan's grandmother. Mark is Ingrid's father. He loves hip hop music, and his cat's name is Tiger. Bob is Mark's father. Suzanne and Mark are geologists. Suzanne is Mark's sister. Suzanne is Julie's aunt. Julie's favorite color is blue. Greg is an actor. He's in movies and on TV shows. He's famous. Greg is Colin's uncle. Annette is a singer. She sings jazz music. She's great! Her dog's name is Duke. It's a black dog. Bob is a cake decorator. His cakes are delicious. He's Ingrid's grandfather. He's Suzanne's father. Christine is a zoologist. She is Colin's mother. Julie and Ingrid are Colin's sisters.

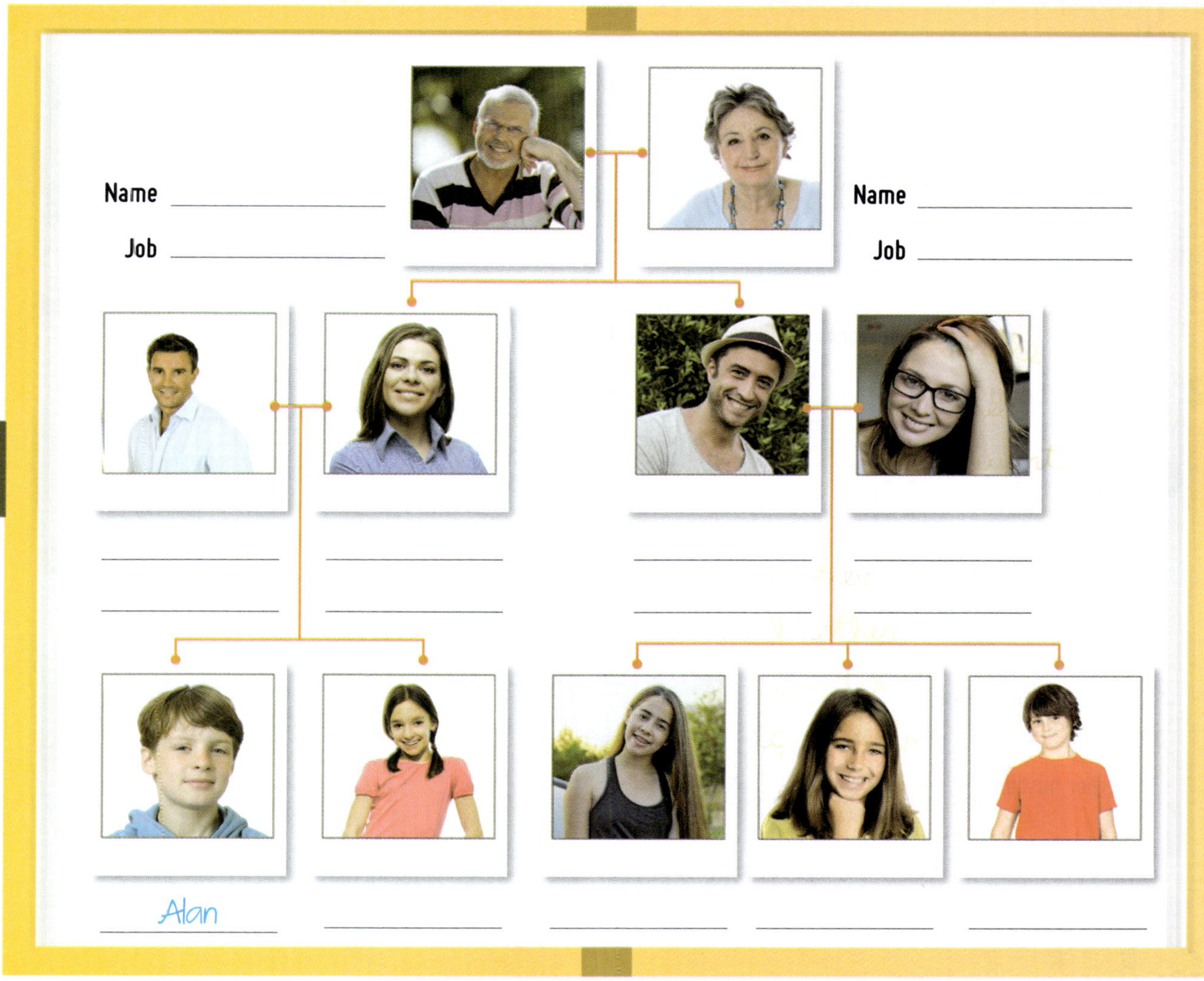

4. Look at **Activity 3**. Write about your family then talk to a classmate about it.

____

____

____

WORKBOOK, 117

CLIL ART

LANGUAGE TIP

To talk about the son/daughter of your son/daughter, we say **grandson** and **granddaughter**. To talk about your grandparents' parents, we say **great-grandfather** and **great-grandmother**.

GRAMMAR

1. Listen and practice. Then read the sentences from the *Grammar* box. 21

grandfather grandmother husband wife son daughter

grandparents (grandfather + grandmother) parents (husband + wife)

2. Answer the questions.

BE (YES-NO QUESTIONS)

Is he	my your his her our their Natasha's	son?	**Yes, he is.** **No, he isn't.**
Are they	my your his her our their Natasha's	parents?	**Yes, they are.** **No, they aren't.**

1  ✔

Is he her husband?

Yes, he is.

2  ✔

Are they their parents?

____

3  ✗

Is he their brother?

____

4  ✔

Is she his wife?

____

5  ✗

Are they her grandparents?

____

LESSON 3

FAMILIES IN ART

Editora de arte

3. Number the masterpieces from 1–4 in the order you like them.

4

Vincent van Gogh. 1890. Potlood op papier. Van Gogh Museum, Amsterdam

Henri Rousseau. *The Wedding Party*, 1905.

This is an oil painting of a French couple on their wedding day. The husband and wife are with their families. Look at the dog! Who is sitting on the tree stump?

1

Dorothea Lange. *Migrant Mother*, 1936.

This interesting black and white photograph is by an American photographer, Dorothea Lange. It's from 1936, and it's a picture of a mother, Florence Owens Thompson, and two daughters.

2

Nikolai Filatov. *Family Monument*, 2008.

This is a bronze sculpture in Saransk, Russia. It's of a man, a woman, and three children. Are the man and woman the parents? Are the children boys or girls?

3

Henri J. F. Rousseau. c. 1905. Oil on canvas. Musee de l'Orangerie, Paris

Vincent van Gogh. *Couple Walking Arm in Arm with a Child in the Rain*, 1890.

This is a pencil drawing by Vincent van Gogh, a famous artist from the Netherlands. The drawing is from 1890. It is a drawing of husband and wife with their son. The weather is terrible!

4. Which masterpiece is it? Write.

1. A drawing of parents and their son: Couple Walking Arm in Arm with a Child in the Rain
2. A photograph of a mother with her two daughters: ______
3. A sculpture of parents with their children: ______
4. A painting with parents, grandparents, and a husband and wife: ______

5. Look at the picture and talk about the question.
These are 3D models of a family in Korea. It's a mother and father with their daughter.
Is this art?

Korean family, 2016.

WORKBOOK, 118

COMMUNICATION

1. Listen and read. (22)

2. Listen and complete the sentences. 23

3. Read. Then write a conversation between your friends.

Marcia: This is my friend, Megan.

Pedro: Hi! Nice to meet you, Megan!

Megan: Hello. Nice to meet you too!

____

____

____

____

____

____

4. Practice introducing your friends to each other.

WORKBOOK, 119

BONUS Magazine

THE BRITISH ROYAL FAMILY

1. Work with a classmate. Circle the correct answer.

1. Where is the United Kingdom?

a. in North America **b.** in Asia **c.** in Europe

LANGUAGE TIP The plural of **wife** is **wives**.

2. Read about the British royal family.

King William I (1066–1087)

William was king for 20 years. He was called "The Conqueror." Queen Elizabeth II is his 25th great-granddaughter.

Hans Holbein the Younger, 1540. Oil on panel. Palazzo Barberini, Roma

King Henry VIII (1509–1547)

Henry VIII was king for 37 years. He had six wives.

National Maritime Museum, London

Queen Elizabeth I (1558–1603)

Elizabeth I was queen for 44 years. She was Henry VIII's daughter.

LANGUAGE TIP When talking about kings and queens, we pronounce William I as **William the First**. We pronounce George II as **George the Second**.

Edwin Landseer. 1840-43. Oil on canvas. Royal Collection Trust, UK

Queen Victoria (1837-1901)

Victoria was queen for 63 years. The British Empire was very big at that time. Her husband was Prince Albert.

Princess Diana (born in 1961-died in 1997)

Prince William is Queen Elizabeth's grandson. His mother was Lady Diana Spencer.

Queen Elizabeth II (1952-present)

Elizabeth II has been queen for over 65 years. She has three sons and one daughter.

Prince Charles (born in 1948), Prince of Wales

Prince Charles is Queen Elizabeth's son. His first wife was Lady Diana Spencer (1961-1997). His second wife is Camilla, Duchess of Cornwall. He has two sons, Prince William and Prince Harry.

Prince William (born in 1982), Duke of Cambridge, and his family

William's wife is Catherine, Duchess of Cambridge. William and Catherine are the parents of Prince George and Princess Charlotte. Prince George is Queen Elizabeth's great-grandson. George will be King George VII one day.

Camilla (born in 1947), Duchess of Cornwall

3. Match.

1. Prince Albert's wife — [ ] Prince George
2. Prince George's great-grandmother — [ ] Queen Elizabeth I
3. Henry VIII's daughter — [1] Queen Victoria
4. Prince William's son — [ ] Queen Elizabeth II

4. Read. Then circle *True* or *False*.

1. Prince William is Prince Harry's brother. — True / False
2. Princess Charlotte is Prince William's daughter. — True / False
3. Prince William is Queen Elizabeth II's grandmother. — True / False
4. Prince George is Prince Harry's son. — True / False

Editoria de arte

REVIEW 1

VOCABULARY

1. Unscramble the words.

1 

irnsge

singer

2 

stogoleig

3 

urot igued

4 

trachetci

5 

nvairnaretei

6 

istanobt

2. Number the dialogue 1–6 in the correct order.

GRAMMAR

3. **Write their real jobs.**

1.

She's not a nutritionist.

She's a cake decorator.

2.

____

____

3.

____

____

4. **Complete the sentences.**

uncle
son
~~parents~~
daughter

1. My mother and father are my parents.
2. My father's brother is my _______________.
3. My father is my grandfather's _______________.
4. My sister is my parent's _______________.

READING

5. **Read about Prince Andrew. Circle the correct alternatives.**

This is Prince Andrew. He's a prince, and he's a pilot too. His parents are Queen Elizabeth II and Prince Philip. His grandfather was King George VI. He is Prince Charles's brother.

Prince Andrew has two daughters. Their names are Beatrice and Eugenie. They aren't queens. They are princesses. Their mother is Sarah Ferguson. Prince Andrew and Sarah Ferguson are not husband and wife now.

1. Prince Andrew is Queen Elizabeth's ...
   a. mother. **c.** son. (circled)
   b. father. **d.** grandmother.

2. Prince Philip is Prince Andrew's ...
   a. uncle. **c.** aunt.
   b. daughter. **d.** father.

3. Prince Andrew is King George VI's ...
   a. grandmother. **c.** grandfather.
   b. grandson. **d.** grandparents.

4. Sarah Ferguson isn't Prince Andrew's ... now
   a. wife. **c.** granddaughter.
   b. daughter. **d.** sister.

Circle.

1. Which unit was more interesting?
   Unit 1 (Cool Jobs!) / Unit 2 (Family Fun)
2. Which unit was more difficult?
   Unit 1 (Cool Jobs!) / Unit 2 (Family Fun)

PUZZLES, 102

UNIT 3

MY THINGS

VOCABULARY

1. Listen and practice. 24

1 
backpack

2 
notebook

3

ID card

4

wallet

5

cell phone

6

video game

7

laptop

8

tablet

9

keys

10

pencil case

25 PRONUNCIATION

Consonant at the end of a word

- notebook
- tablet
- backpack
- laptop
- ID card

2. Read and write the words. Then listen and check. 26

3. Write.

1

3

2

4

1. What is it? It's a wallet.
   What is it? It's a key.
2. What are they? They're ____________.
3. What is it? It's a ____________.
4. What is it? It's a ____________.

WORKBOOK, 120

GRAMMAR

1. Look at the conversation. Then read the examples in the *Grammar* box.

BE (WH-QUESTIONS)

What **is** it?	It**'s** a key. It**'s** an ID card.
What **are** they?	They**'re** pencil cases. They**'re** backpacks.

2. Circle the correct options.

1. What is it? *It's* / *They're* a notebook.
2. What are they? *It's* / *They're* tablets.
3. What *is* / *are* they? They're wallets.
4. What *is* / *are* it? It's a backpack.
5. What *is it* / *are they*? They're keys.
6. What *is it* / *are they*? It's a video game.

3. Write *What is it?* or *What are they?* Then match the questions and answers to the correct pictures.

1. ________
It's a notebook.
2. ________
They're tablets.
3. ________
It's a wallet.
4. ________
They're notebooks.
5. ________
They're wallets.
6. ________
It's a pencil case.

READING

LANGUAGE TIP

Some words are very similar in English and Portuguese. These are called **cognates**. If you see a new word and it looks like one in your language, it probably means the same thing.

4. Read the interview.

All Tech Webcast

Allison: Good evening and welcome to All Tech, our webcast about technological innovations. Today we're talking to Erica Driver, a tech designer.
Erica: Hello, Allison. Look at this.
Allison: What is it?
Erica: It's a cell phone.
Allison: A cell phone! Really?
Erica: Yes, it's a Projector Phone. It's for 2023, not now.
Allison: It's modern and very cool!
Erica: Look.
Allison: What are they?
Erica: They're ID cards. They're part of our biometric identification program.
Allison: Biometric identification? What is it?
Erica: ID cards are important, and it's a modern ID card.
Allison: Wow!
Erica: This is great. Look!
Allison: What is it? A backpack?
Erica: Yes, a backpack for the future. It's a cell phone too.
Allison: A backpack and a cell phone?
Erica: Yes. Your books are in here, and here is your cell phone.
Allison: Incredible!
Erica: And there's a video game here. Look!
Allison: Really? A backpack, a cell phone, and a video game?
Erica: And an ID card! But it's for 2038, not now. Your son and daughter will love it!

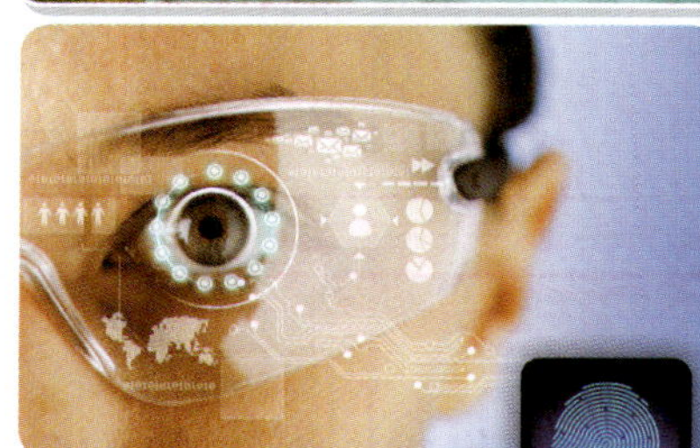

5. Answer the questions and then check ✔ your opinion.

1 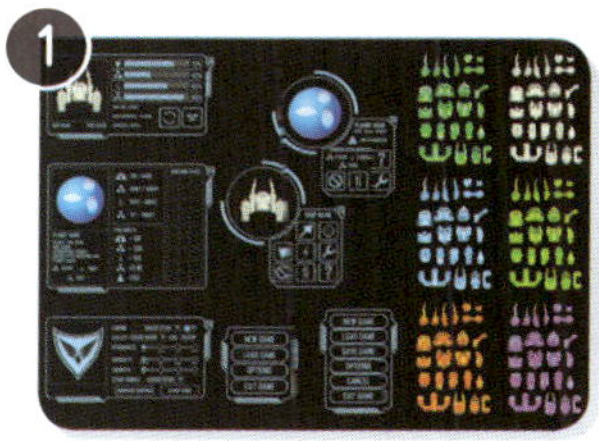

3 

2 

4 

YOUR OPINION

	❤	👍	😕
1. What is it? *It's a video game*.			
2. What is it? ______.			
3. What is it? ______.			
4. What is it? ______.			

WORKBOOK, 121

CLIL

HISTORY

GRAMMAR

1. Listen and practice. Then read the examples in the *Grammar* box. 27

1

old

2

new

3

heavy

4

light

5

big

6

small

7

long

8

short

9

thick

10

thin

DEMONSTRATIVE PRONOUNS: *THIS, THAT, THESE, THOSE*

This desk is big.

That desk is small.

These books are thick.

Those books are thin.

2. Circle **this**, **that**, **these**, or **those**. Then complete the sentences with **is** or **are** and the words in the box.

heavy ~~big~~ small new

1

2

3

4

1. *These* / *That* fish is big.
2. *This* / *That* bird ______.
3. *This* / *These* laptops ______.
4. *Those* / *This* cat ______.

CAMERAS: PAST AND PRESENT

3. Read and listen. 28

1 This is an antique camera, from about 150 **years** ago. It's from 1870. It's very heavy. It takes black and white pictures.

1870

2 This camera is from about a **century** ago, from 1910. Pictures from this camera are in black and white too.

1910

3 This is a 35 mm camera. It's from the 1920s. It's small and light, and it takes good pictures.

1925

4 This is a Polaroid camera. It's from the 1970s. You take a picture and you can get it immediately. It's fun!

1970

5 This camera is from a **decade** ago. It's a digital camera. The pictures can go to your computer quickly.

2005

6 Modern cell phones take great pictures. You can send your pictures to your friends and family. You can put them on the Internet.

Now

7 Doctors use these cameras. They're very small (only 1 mm x 1 mm) and they're very light. They take pictures inside your body.

Now

4. Which camera is it? Read and number the sentences 1–7.

- [3] This camera is from 1910, and it takes black and white pictures.
- [6] This camera is on your cell phone.
- [7] These cameras are very small. Doctors use them.
- [1] This camera is 150 years old. It's heavy.
- [2] This camera takes digital pictures, but it's not a cell phone.
- [5] This is a small, light camera from the 1920s.
- [4] This camera is from the 1970s.

5. Write the highlighted words from **Activity 3**.

1. 12 months: year
2. 10 years: decade
3. 100 years: century

WORKBOOK, 122

COMMUNICATION

1. Look at the advertisements below. What are they about?

a. Technology in the future.
b. Technology in the 1970s and 1980s.
c. Technology now.

2. Listen and read. (29)

This is a video game from 1976. With Super Pong IV, you can play ping-pong (table tennis) and other simple games. You can play it with your family or with your friends. It's fun!

What is that? It's an advertisement for a computer. It's a computer from 1984.

This is a cell phone from 1988. It's heavy. It's 800 grams — almost one kilo! And it's $1,499.

3. Listen and check ✔ the words you hear. (30)

- [ ] portable computers
- [ ] small
- [ ] funny
- [x] old
- [ ] big
- [ ] laptops

4. Listen and practice. 31

5. Read. Then write about your favorite things.

This is my cell phone. It's new and it's great. My mother's laptop isn't new. It's old. My video game is old, but it's awesome.

6. Tell your classmates about your favorite things.

WORKBOOK, 123

BONUS Magazine

Collections

1. **Answer the questions. Then talk to your classmate.**

1. Do you collect something?
2. Do your friends have collections? What do they collect?

2. **Read the article.**

This is Lisa Courtney. She's a Pokémon fan in the UK. She has the world's largest collection of Pokémon memorabilia. Since she was nine years old, Lisa, 26, has collected animals, toys, and clothes from the Japanese animated series. She now has more than 16,000 items.

Lisa said it was love at first sight when she saw a picture of Pikachu in a Nintendo magazine as a young child. Lisa uses her master bedroom to accommodate her massive collection.

She started collecting when she was at school. She was awarded the Guinness world record for largest collection of memorabilia. Lisa searches for Pokémon things to buy and trade on the Internet. She also visits many shops on the weekends. Lisa says she will always collect Pokémon and will never stop because there's always something new to get.

Pokémon Facts

Pokémon was created in 1996, over 20 years ago.
"Pokémon" is short for "Pocket Monsters."
Pokémon are from Japan.
Nintendo makes Pokémon and Mario.
The Pokémon franchise has earned $46 billion.
There are 19 Pokemon movies.

3. **Choose the correct alternative.**

1. Lisa is from ...
   a. the USA.
   b. Japan.
   c. Nintendoland.
   d. The UK.

2. Lisa has a collection of ...
   a. Nintendo stores.
   b. bedrooms.
   c. magazines.
   d. Pokémon memorabilia.

3. Pokémon are from ...
   a. Japan.
   b. China.
   c. Brazil.
   d. the UK.

4. Lisa is ...
   a. nine years old.
   b. 20 years old.
   c. 26 years old.
   d. France.

5. Pokémon is short for ...
   a. Button Monsters.
   b. Poke Monsters.
   c. Pocket Monsters.
   d. Pet Monsters.

6. Lisa buys Pokémon memorabilia ...
   a. in Ireland.
   b. on the Internet.
   c. in Japan.
   d. from her mother.

LANGUAGE TIP

The Japanese language contains many words from other languages, including Portuguese. These are called **loan words**. Here are some examples:
Pão is *pan*; *copo* is *koppu*; *botão* is *botan*.

Other Collections

4. **In your opinion, are these good things to collect? Circle the number of stars based on your preferences.**

coins

caps

stamps

comic books

rocks

teddy bears

clocks

badges

Editoria de arte

UNIT

4 LET'S GO SHOPPING!

LANGUAGE TIP

There are many different types of shoes. For example, **sneakers**, **sandals**, and **pumps** are all common types of shoes.

VOCABULARY

1. Listen and practice. 32

1 
T-shirt

2 
sweatshirt

33 PRONUNCIATION

/s/ and /sh/	
socks	**sh**oes
skirt	**sh**irt
sweatshirt	T-**sh**irt
small	**sh**orts

3 
jeans

4 
jacket

5 
sneakers

6 
skirt

7 
dress

8 
cap

9 
shirt

10 
socks

2. Read. Then write the words.

3. Listen and check. 34

4. Read the sentences. Number the floor plan 1–6.

1. These are the socks.
2. That's the T-shirt and sweatshirt section.
3. The sneakers are in that section.
4. Those are the caps.
5. They're the T-shirts.
6. These are the jackets.

5. Write three things that you would like to buy at this store.

1. ____________
2. ____________
3. ____________

WORKBOOK, 124

GRAMMAR

1. Look at the conversation. Then read the examples in the *Grammar* box.

LANGUAGE TIP

Notice that adjective order is different in English, and not the same as your language. The adjectives come before the noun: **adjective + noun**.

LANGUAGE TIP

When the adjective begins with a vowel, don't forget to use *an*, not *a*. For example:

That's **a** T-shirt. That's **an** ugly T-shirt.
It's **a** skirt. It's **an** expensive skirt.

ADJECTIVE ORDER

That's a **cool** sweatshirt.
That's a **cool red** sweatshirt.

Those are **beautiful** dresses.
Those are **beautiful blue** dresses.

2. Unscramble and write the sentences.

1. a / beautiful / That's / shirt / orange / .
   That's a beautiful orange shirt.
2. white / new / jackets / They're / .
   ____
3. cap / expensive / It's / an / black / .
   ____
4. shoes / They're / pink / ugly / .
   ____
5. It's / sock / long / a / white / .
   ____
6. jeans / blue / They're / beautiful / .
   ____

READING

3. Look at the uniforms in **Activity 4.** Number the sentences 1–5.

1. white socks, blue pants [ ]
2. black shoes, pink dress [ ]
3. white pants, white skirt [1]
4. black caps, black shoes [ ]
5. blue jeans, gray sweatshirt [ ]

LANGUAGE TIP

Jeans and *leggings* are types of *pants*.

4. Read and check ✔ your favorite school uniform.

1 [ ]

This is a white uniform. It's beautiful. This is the boy's uniform. They're white pants and white shoes. The shirt is white too. This is the girl's uniform. They're white socks, white shoes, a white skirt, and a white shirt.

2 [ ]

These are cool blue jackets, white shirts, and black shoes for the boy and the girl. For the boy, they're blue pants and for the girl, it's a red, white, and blue skirt with white socks. Awesome!

3 [ ]

Black! For the boy and the girl, the uniform is black. They're black caps, black shirts, black pants, black jackets, and black shoes. It's very nice.

4 [ ]

This is very interesting. For the girl, it's a pink dress and pink shoes. For the boy, it's a pink shirt, pink pants, and black shoes. It's great!

5 [ ]

Blue jeans, white T-shirts, and a cool gray sweatshirt. And your shoes – red, yellow, blue, black... This is a great uniform. It's cheap, and it's cool.

WORKBOOK, 125

CLIL MATH

GRAMMAR

Editoria de arte

1. Listen and practice. Then read the examples in the *Grammar* box. 35

twenty-one

twenty-two

twenty-three

thirty

forty

fifty

sixty

seventy

eighty

ninety

one hundred

HOW MUCH...? (PRICES)

How much is the blue cap?	It's twenty-three dollars.
How much are the red shoes?	They're one hundred dollars.

LANGUAGE TIP

We can say prices in dollars and cents in any of the following ways:
twenty-two dollars and thirty-three cents
twenty-two dollars, thirty-three cents
twenty-two dollars, thirty-three

LANGUAGE TIP

Some items of clothing are treated as if they were plural because usually they are made up of two parts. For example, ***jeans***, ***pants***, or ***leggings***.

2. Write the prices in words.

1. How much is the yellow cap?

   It's twenty-one dollars.

2. How much are the green shoes?

   ____

3. How much are the blue jeans?

   ____

SPENDING MONEY

3. Read and listen. 36

WHAT TEENAGERS BUY

Accessories 10%

Video games 8%

Other stuff 8%

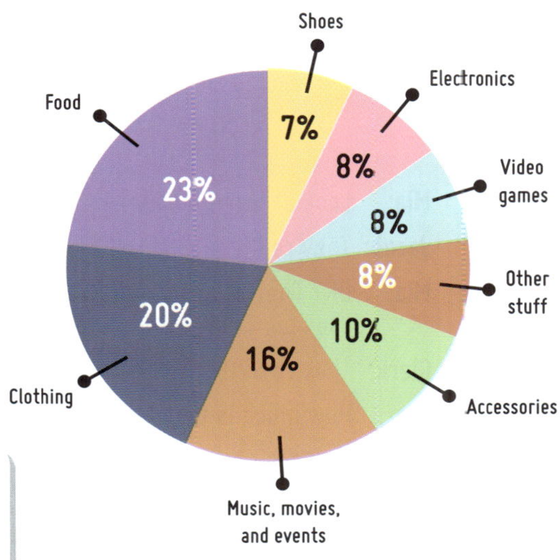

Clothing 20%

Electronics 8%

Shoes 7%

Food 23%

Music, movies, and events 16%

This is a pie chart. It shows what teenagers in the USA **buy** with their **allowances**. The chart shows percentages. The number one thing is food (23%). This means that they spend 23 dollars of every 100 dollars at restaurants and cafes. Their favorite is fast food. Clothing is the number two item (20%). The most popular items of clothing are jeans and sports clothes. Teenagers spend 16% of their **money** on music, movies, and events. Accessories like sunglasses and ear buds (10%) are also popular. Teenagers like video games (8%) and electronics (8%) too. And teenagers spend 7% of their money on shoes. Sports shoes are expensive. They spend 8% of their allowances on other stuff.

Editoria de arte

4. Complete the sentences with highlighted words from **Activity 3**.

1. Euros, dollars, and reais are kinds of ____________ .
2. The money you get every week is your ____________ .
3. Look at these shoes. Let's ____________ them!

> % means percent
> 30% = 30/100
> 30% = 0.3

5. Kate's allowance is $200 a month. Based on the information from **Activity 3**, how much does she spend on each item?

Food	$ 46	Music, movies, events	$ ___	Video games	$ ___	Shoes	$ ___
Clothing	$ ___	Accessories	$ ___	Electronics	$ ___	Other	$ ___

WORKBOOK, 126

COMMUNICATION

1. Look at the pictures in **Activity 2.** Check ✔ the things you see.

1. ☑ shoes
2. ☐ caps
3. ☐ sweatshirts
4. ☐ T-shirts
5. ☐ socks

2. Listen and read. 37

Mia: Look at these T-shirts!

Jacob: They're OK.

Mia: OK? They're beautiful. Excuse me, how much are the blue T-shirts?

Clerk: They're $20.

Mia: How much is that pink one?

Clerk: It's $18.

Mia: This pink T-shirt is beautiful, but the blue ones are really cool. The yellow one is nice too.

Jacob: Mia!

Mia: OK. I'd like this pink one, please.

Clerk: OK! Here you are.

Mia: Thank you!

Jacob: Look at these shoes!

Mia: They're OK.

Jacob: No, they're really cool. Excuse me, how much are these black shoes?

Clerk: The black ones are $99.

Jacob: $99? How much are those orange shoes?

Clerk: The orange ones are $98.

Mia: The orange ones are ugly.

Jacob: No, they're great.

Mia: Jacob!

Jacob: I'd like the orange ones, please.

Clerk: Here you are.

Jacob: Thank you.

3. Listen and write the price you hear. 38

1. How much is the yellow T-shirt?

____

2. How much are the green shoes?

____

4. Listen and practice. 39

5. Read. Then write a conversation about something you'd like to buy.

Girl: Look at these dresses! They're beautiful. How much is the white one?

Clerk: It's $68.

Girl: How much is the green one?

Clerk: It's $57.

Girl: I'd like the green one.

Clerk: Here you are.

Girl: Thank you.

6. Offer your school supplies to your classmates. Talk about them.

WORKBOOK, 127

BONUS Magazine

SHOPPING ONLINE

1. Read the advertisements.

1

Zipbuds have a zippy design and are very flexible. Zipbuds have award-winning sound. They have an integrated microphone too.

2

This is one of our favorite drones. It's the most reliable and most enjoyable little drone we have. It records the flight on the camera. You can enjoy your recorded movies later. If you want to, you can put them on YouTube!

3

Let the USB Spaceman light the way! Plug in and open the visor up to turn the light on. The light plugs into a USB port. Fully adjustable cord.

4

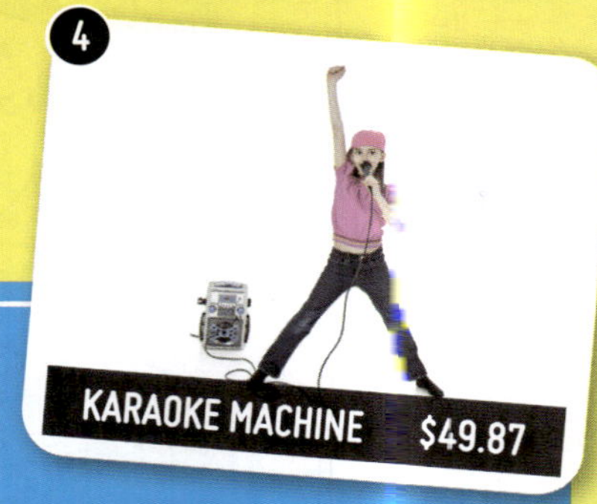

This karaoke machine is for any teen who loves singing. There are colorful lights and many sound options! The best part about this machine is that you can plug a phone in.

Connect to the Laser Keyboard, place on a flat surface and watch the red laser keys appear! This laser keyboard can also be used as a power bank.

For teens, playing sports can be a big deal. This makes a great gift for teens. Improve agility, or quickness for any game, from football to tennis. This is a great kit for training at home.

This 23-piece instrument kit is an awesome gift for teens interested in learning different musical instruments. There are 23 instruments from around the world. It also comes with an instructional DVD.

Art class can be one of the best school subjects a teen can take in middle or high school. This media set allows for creative artwork in many forms, from paints to pencils.

2. What is it? Find the words from the websites and write the products.

1. It's creative.
   art kit
2. It's great for training.
   ______
3. It can be used as a power bank.
   ______
4. It's reliable and enjoyable.
   ______
5. It comes with a DVD.
   ______
6. It's for teens who love singing.
   ______
7. It plugs into a USB port.
   ______
8. They are very flexible.
   ______

REVIEW 2

1. Write the words in pairs of opposites.

new	heavy
long	light
big	old
small	short

2. Write the answers to the sums.

1. There are twenty-six red pencil cases and sixteen blue pencil cases. How many pencil cases are there?

2. There are sixty caps. There are green caps and blue caps. Twenty-two caps are blue. How many green caps are there?

3. Jaden's allowance is six dollars and fifty cents a week. How much is his allowance per year?

3. Complete the sentences with words from the box.

awesome	Here	It's	much	shoes	They're

GRAMMAR

4. Write sentences with *this, that, these,* and *those.*

1 

That is a backpack.

2 

3 

4 

5 

6 

READING

5. Read. Circle the correct alternatives.

This is Carl. He is 13 years old. That is his stamp collection. There are 300 stamps. That's a big collection. There are old ones and new ones. That's an old one from 1840. It's a Penny Black from England. It's his favorite.

Emily is 13, and she has a collection too. It's a T-shirt collection. There are 70 T-shirts from all around the world. Her favorite T-shirt is a white and yellow one from Japan. It's a manga T-shirt. Emily has a wish list. There is a T-shirt on her wish list: a T-shirt of her favorite American singer.

1. Carl's collection is ...
   a. 13 years old.
   b. a stamp collection.
2. Carl's favorite stamp is ...
   a. a manga.
   b. a Penny Black.
3. Emily's collection is ...
   a. a T-shirt collection.
   b. a manga collection.
4. Emily's favorite T-shirt is ...
   a. white and yellow.
   b. from England.
5. On Emily's wish list there is ...
   a. a Penny Black T-shirt.
   b. a T-shirt of her favorite singer.

Circle.

1. Which unit was more interesting? Unit 3 (My Things) / Unit 4 (Let's Go Shopping!)
2. Which unit was more difficult? Unit 3 (My Things) / Unit 4 (Let's Go Shopping!)

PUZZLES, 103 BOARD GAME, 106-107

UNIT 5

HOME SWEET HOME

VOCABULARY

1. Listen and practice. 40

ROOMS

1 
living room

2 
bedroom

Hi! I'm Lucas. I'm a student and this is my house. I am in the (1) yard now. This is our cat, Sally. Sally is old. She's fifteen now. Let's go inside the house.

This is my favorite room. It's the (4) ______________. There a big green (5) ______________ and a (6) ______________. Those are my parents. My father is a nutritionist. My mother is an architect. Don't sleep, Dad!

Who's he? He's my brother, Kyle. That's our big (2) ______________. It's in the (3) ______________. That's a hamburger. Yum! That looks good! That's our dog, Frosty.

There's a (7) ______________ in the (8) ______________. There are five chairs, too. That's my grandmother. She's a botanist. She's sixty-six years old. Good evening, Grandma!

kitchen

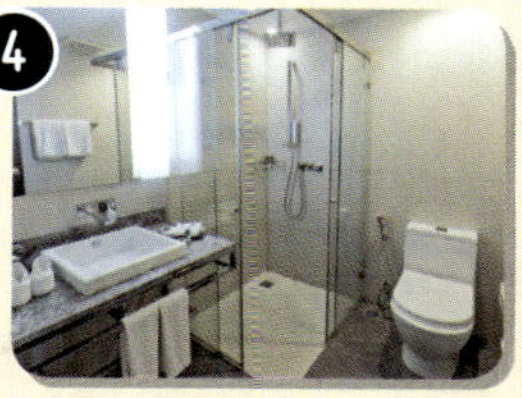
bathroom

dining room

yard

FURNITURE

sofa

TV

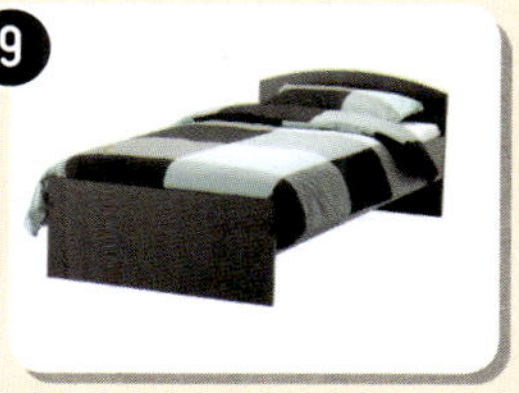
bed

table

fridge

bookshelf

2. Read and write the words. Then listen and check. 41

42 **PRONUNCIATION**

Words ending with /m/

Be sure to pronounce the m sound at the end of these words. Be careful that you don't replace the m sound with an n sound.

- room
- bedroom
- bathroom
- living room
- dining room

3. Write about your home.

ROOM	WHAT'S IN THE ROOM?
Living room	
Kitchen	
Dining room	
Bathroom	
Bedroom	
Yard	

WORKBOOK, 128

GRAMMAR

1. Look at the conversation. Then read the examples in the *Grammar* box.

THERE IS / THERE ARE	
SINGULAR	PLURAL
There is a sofa.	**There are** two sofas.
There isn't a TV.	**There aren't** TVs.
Is there a sofa? Yes, **there is.** / No, **there isn't.**	**Are there** sofas? Yes, **there are.** / No, **there aren't.**

Editoria de arte

2. Circle the correct word.

1. There *is* / *are* a sofa in our living room.
2. There *is* / *are* three chairs in the dining room.
3. *Is* / *Are* there a fridge in the kitchen?
4. There *isn't* / *aren't* TVs in our bedrooms.
5. *Is* / *Are* there two beds in your bedroom?
6. There *isn't* / *aren't* a table in our yard.

LANGUAGE TIP
We often abbreviate *there is* to *there's*.

3. Complete the blanks with *is*, *isn't*, *are*, or *aren't*.

1. There __is__ a big sofa in our living room. It's great!
2. ____ there a bookshelf in your dining room?
3. ____ there two beds in your bedroom? No, there aren't.
4. There ____ two chairs in the bedroom. I can see only one.
5. There ____ a table in our kitchen. It's in the dining room.
6. There ____ two chairs in my bedroom.

READING

4. Look at the text in **Activity 5** and write *Yes* or *No.*

1. It's a blog entry. Yes
2. It's a social media page. ______

5. Listen and read the text. 43

Nicole's blog

Hi! My name is Nicole. I'm eleven years old. I'm a student. Luke is my brother. He's twelve and he's a student too. My mother is a doctor, and my father is a teacher. These are their books. There's a big bookcase in their bedroom. There's a TV in the living room, but there aren't TVs in our bedrooms. That's OK. Books are cool, and there are books in my bedroom. There's a big bookshelf in my bedroom, and my favorite book is *Astronauts*. In our house, there's a table and there are four chairs in our dining room. There's a small table and a big fridge in our kitchen. This is our dog, Duke. He's gray and white. And this is our cat, Princess. She's black and brown. They're friends.

6. Write **T** (true) or **F** (false).

F 1. Nicole is twelve years old.

☐ 2. There's a big bookcase in Nicole's parents' bedroom.

☐ 3. There are two TVs in the living room.

☐ 4. There are books in Nicole's bedroom.

☐ 5. There are four chairs in their dining room.

☐ 6. There's a big table in their kitchen.

7. Answer the questions.

1. How old is Nicole? She's 11 years old.
2. Is there a TV in their living room? ______
3. Are there TVs in their bedrooms? ______
4. Are there books in Nicole's bedroom? ______
5. Is there a sofa in their dining room? ______
6. Are there six chairs in their dining room? ______

WORKBOOK, 129

CLIL HISTORY

GRAMMAR

Editoria de arte

1. Listen and practice. Then read the examples in the *Grammar* box. 44

1 
castle

2 
tower

3 
door

4 
wall

5 
window

6 
knight

7 
moat

8 
hall

9 
drawbridge

10 
flag

HOW MANY + THERE IS / THERE ARE

How many towers **are there**?	**There are** no towers.
	There's one. / **There's** one tower.
	There are two. / **There are** two towers.

2. Answer the questions.

1. How many red flags are there?
   There are three red flags.
2. How many white knights are there?
   ____
3. How many black towers are there?
   ____
4. How many brown horses are there?
   ____

THE TOWER OF LONDON

LANGUAGE TIP

The word **beefeaters** is a nickname from a time when these guards were paid with pieces of beef.

3. Read. Then underline *There's* and *There are*.

Let's visit the Tower of London!
The Tower of London is a big **castle**. It's from 1080. That was the time of King William I, The Conqueror. The walls are very thick and old.

There are twenty towers and many windows. The towers are very tall. There's a **moat**. There are lots of rooms and halls in the castle. There are big rooms and small rooms.

There are **beefeaters** in the Tower of London. They aren't knights. They look after the Tower of London. Their blue and red uniforms are expensive.

There are black birds in the Tower of London. They are called The Ravens of the Tower. They are big.

There's a **drawbridge** in the Tower of London. This one is not old. It's new. It's very heavy.

4. Write **T** (true) or **F** (false).

F **1.** The Tower of London is a small house.

2. There's a moat.

3. There are nineteen towers.

4. The birds in the Tower of London are black.

5. The beefeaters' clothes are green.

6. There's one drawbridge.

5. How are castles and houses or apartment buildings different? Write sentences.

There are no towers on a house. There are towers on a castle.

WORKBOOK, 130

COMMUNICATION

1. Read Tina and Jack's conversation. Then circle the correct option.

Tina
online

This is my family's new house.

Oh really?

Yes, look at my pictures.

It's a boat!

Tina
online

Yes, it's a houseboat. It's in California.

Cool!

There's a small kitchen. There's a table in the dining room. There are two chairs too.

Wow! It's small.

Yes, it is.

How many bedrooms are there?

There are two bedrooms. There's a small bed and a bookshelf in my bedroom. There's a big bed and a TV in my parent's bedroom.

Great!

There isn't a yard, but there's water and there are fish!

Editoria de arte

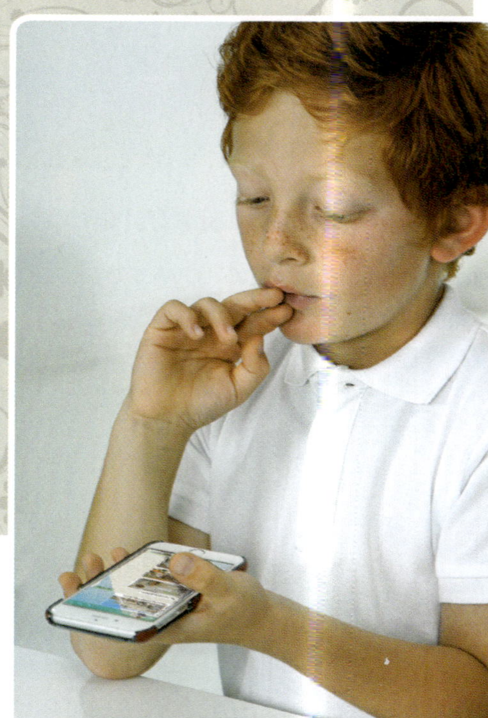

1. Tina's house is *a houseboat* / *an apartment*.
2. There *is* / *isn't* a kitchen on the houseboat.
3. There *are* / *aren't* two tables in the dining room.

2. Listen and match about Jack's house. 45

1. Where is Jack's house?
2. How many bedrooms are there?
3. How many bathrooms are there?
4. Is there a moat?

- [ ] No, there isn't.
- [ ] There are five.
- [1] It's in Ireland.
- [ ] There are fourteen.

3. Listen and practice. 46

47 PRONUNCIATION

We can say **really** in different ways. All of them express interest in what the other person is saying.

- Really.
- Really!
- Really?

4. Read. Then write about your dream house.

In my dream house, there's a big sofa in the living room. There are three TVs. There are video games, and there's a robot! There are four bedrooms, three bathrooms, and a big kitchen. There isn't a yard.

____

____

____

____

____

____

5. Tell a classmate about your dream house. Your classmate should use expressions from **Activity 1.**

WORKBOOK, 131

BONUS Magazine

Cool HOUSES

1. **Answer the questions. Then talk to your classmate.**

1. Are these houses cool?
2. Are there any interesting houses where you live?

LANGUAGE TIP

When talking about things we can say something is **-shaped** or **shaped like something**. We can also say that **it looks like something**.

2. **Read. Then number the houses 1–8 in the order you like them.**

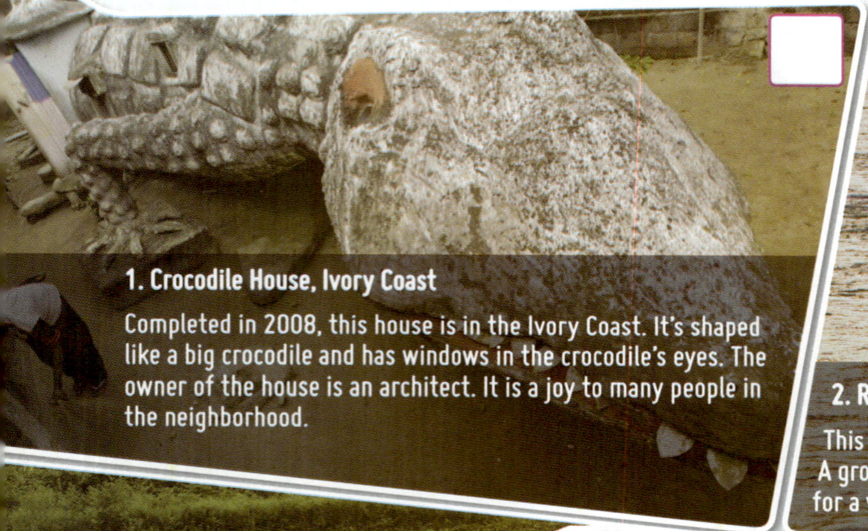

1. Crocodile House, Ivory Coast

Completed in 2008, this house is in the Ivory Coast. It's shaped like a big crocodile and has windows in the crocodile's eyes. The owner of the house is an architect. It is a joy to many people in the neighborhood.

2. River House, Serbia

This house stands on a rock in the river Drina in Serbia. A group of young men decided the rock was an ideal place for a very small house.

3. Soccer Ball House, Japan

This ball-shaped house was designed in 2006, in Gifu, Japan. The 32-sided sphere floats, has the structural strength to resist earthquakes, and costs under $15,000.

4. Airplane House, Lebanon

This is an airplane house in the village of Miziara, Lebanon. It's shaped like an Airbus A380. That's a big airplane. There are windows and wings!

5. Casa de Pedra, Brazil

This is a house in São Paulo. It is called the Casa de Pedra or House of Stone. The owner built it himself out of every imaginable kind of object. Many people come to visit this beautiful house.

ar House, Austria

s car-shaped house is in Austria. It looks like a car, but it is not bile! The house accommodates two generations of a family. It tures sustainable technologies and energy saving systems.

7. Toilet House, South Korea

This house is in Suwon, Korea. It was built in 2007 by Sim Jae Duck, the chairman of the World Toilet Association. The house cost $1.1 million to build. The toilet shaped house has three toilets! The house is now a Toilet Museum.

8. Transparent House, Japan

This see-through house is located in Tokyo, Japan. The 85 square meter transparent house was inspired by people in the past who inhabited trees. There is plenty of daylight, but no privacy here.

3. Which house is it? Write the numbers.

[ ] 1. This house is shaped like a soccer ball.

[ ] 2. This house is on a rock in a river.

[ ] 3. This house looks like a big toilet.

[ ] 4. This house is airplane-shaped.

[ ] 5. This house is transparent.

[ ] 6. This house is shaped like a car.

[1] 7. This house's owner is an architect.

[ ] 8. This house is in Brazil.

4. Complete the table with the numbers of the houses from **Activity 2**.

These houses are crazy.		These houses are beautiful.	
These houses are awesome.		These houses are ugly.	

UNIT 6

SPORTS WORLD!

VOCABULARY

1. Listen and practice. 48

SPORTS

1 soccer

2 baseball

LANGUAGE TIP

In American English:
soccer **football**

Hi, I'm Miranda and I'm a (1) ___soccer___ player. In soccer, we can run and we can kick the ball. That's my favorite player. She's from Washington. Look at that! What a great goal!

Hi. I'm André and I play (2) ____________. In this sport, we can play singles or doubles. We can hit the ball with a racket. To serve, (3) ____________ the ball up high and hit it hard.

Hi. I'm Jennifer Craven. Welcome to SSC. That's the Super Sports Channel.

I'm Jack Stone. Let's look at our favorite sports here on SSC.

I play (4) ____________. It's very fast and very fun. It's also called "ping-pong." We can (5) ____________ the ball over the net. The racket is called a "paddle."

LANGUAGE TIP

There are sports and activities that we **do** or **practice** such as martial arts. All of the sports here are sports we **play**. For instance, **play tennis** or **play soccer**.

3 
volleyball

4 
tennis

5 
basketball

6 
table tennis

VERBS

7 
run

8 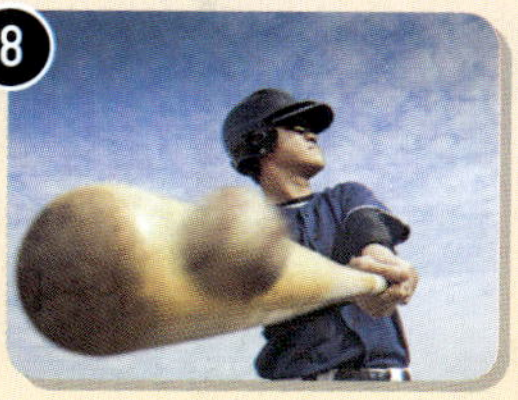
hit

9 
throw

10 
jump

11 
catch

12 
kick

(6) __________ is a great sport. There are five players on a team. In this sport, the players can (7) __________ up and down the court. They can jump up and throw the ball into the hoop. It's a fun sport.

Hi. I'm Alana and this is my sport, (8) __________. It's a really fun team sport. There are six people on each team. The players can (9) __________ up and hit the ball over the net.

My name is Brandon. This is my sport. It's (0) __________. In this sport, we can throw the ball, we can hit the ball with a bat, and we can (11) __________ the ball in a glove.

2. **Read and write the words. Then listen and check.** 49

3. **Match the descriptions with the sports.**

1. You can play this on a table. It's a very fast sport.
2. Players can run, jump, and throw a big orange ball.
3. There are five people on a team. They jump up and hit the ball over a net!
4. There are two teams. You can kick the ball at the goal.

[ ] basketball

[ ] volleyball

[ ] soccer

[1] table tennis

4. **Do a sports survey of your classmates.**

WORKBOOK, 132

GRAMMAR

1. Read the conversation. Then look at the examples in the *Grammar* box.

50 PRONUNCIATION

***Can* is pronounced in different ways. You can sometimes hear:**

I *can* play tennis.
/kn/

And sometimes:

Yes, I *can*.
/kan/

CAN

Can	I you he she it we they	jump?

Yes,	I you he she it we they	**can.**	No,	I you he she it we they	**can't.**

LANGUAGE TIP

We use **can** and **can't** for two things:

- abililty

He **can** kick the ball.

- permission

You **can't** kick the ball in basketball.

2. Circle the correct option.

1. Basketball players *can* / *can't* kick the ball.
2. My dog *can* / *can't* catch tennis balls. She's great!
3. My brother is a baby. He *can* / *can't* run.
4. My great-grandfather is very old. He *can* / *can't* jump.
5. Volleyball players *can* / *can't* hit the ball.
6. You *can* / *can't* throw the ball in baseball, but not in soccer.

READING

3. Read the description of Ultimate. Then write **T** (true) or **F** (false).

Hi! I'm Wyatt Green and Ultimate is my favorite sport. Ultimate? It can be "Ultimate Frisbee" or "Frisbee football," but to me and my friends, it's "Ultimate."

This is an Ultimate team. There are seven players on a team. Teams can be boys, teams can be girls, or teams can be mixed: boys and girls.

There are two goals, or "end zones." Can you catch the Frisbee in the end zone? One point!

You can throw the Frisbee, but you can't run with it!

There are no referees in Ultimate. There is "spirit of the game." What's that? Play with respect. Be honest.

On defense, you can hit the Frisbee down. The Frisbee is your team's Frisbee now!

Ultimate is a great sport. It's cheap, and you can run, jump, throw, and catch. Go play Ultimate and have fun!

1. Ultimate is Wyatt's favorite sport. T
2. There are fourteen players on a team.
3. You can't run with the Frisbee.
4. There are two end zones.

WORKBOOK, 133

CLIL

HEALTH/PHYSICAL EDUCATION

Crédito das ilustrações: Casa de Ideias

GRAMMAR

IMPERATIVES

Eat good food! Don't kick the TV!

Editoria de arte

1. Listen and practice. Then read the examples in the *Grammar* box. 51

eat good food

exercise

get enough sleep

drink water

keep clean

have fun

2. Complete the sentences with expressions from the box.

1. Don't run in the bathroom.
2. ____________ a soccer ball in the living room.
3. ____________ your laptop.
4. ____________ on your bed.
5. ____________ games all day.
6. ____________ basketball in the kitchen.

Don't hit
~~Don't run~~
Don't play vide
Don't jump
Don't play
Don't kick

Six Healthy Steps

3. **Read and listen. Then circle the correct alternative.** 52

These are six steps to health. Do these things every day.

Step 1

Exercise in your yard, at a park, community center, or gym. Do it every day. Play your favorite sport. But first, stretch!

Step 2

Keep clean. It's healthy. Wash your hands and brush your teeth.

Step 3

Drink water every morning, afternoon, and evening. Water is important for health.

Step 4

Have fun with your family and friends. You can play board games, card games, or video games.

Step 5

Eight to ten hours of sleep is good for you. Get enough sleep. It's important to rest.

Step 6

Eat good food every day. Fruit and vegetables are good for you.

1. Have fun:	**a.** sleep all day **b.** play baseball
2. Exercise:	**a.** read a book **b.** run
3. Get enough sleep:	**a.** get six hours sleep **b.** get nine hours sleep
4. Drink water:	**a.** drink water every day **b.** drink water on Wednesday and Sunday

4. **Make a healthy activity diary for this week.**

WORKBOOK, 134

COMMUNICATION

1. Look at the pictures. Check ✓ the activities you see.

- [x] hip-hop dance
- [ ] Ultimate
- [ ] yoga
- [ ] baseball
- [ ] football
- [ ] basketball
- [ ] table tennis

2. Listen and read. 53

Dad: You can play football.

Noah: Football? I can't play football.

Dad: Yes, you can.

Noah: No, I'm bad at football. I can't throw the ball, I can't run fast, and I can't catch the ball.

Dad: But football is fun.

Noah: No, I'm not good at it.

Dad: OK. What about basketball?

Noah: Basketball? I'm not good at basketball.

Dad: Look! Trampoline basketball.

Noah: Trampoline basketball?

Dad: It's fun. There's a basketball and a trampoline. You can jump, you can throw ...

Noah: No, I'm not good at that.

Dad: OK. Hip-hop!

Noah: Hip-hop dance? I'm bad at that.

Dad: There's good music. It's good exercise. I'm good at hip-hop.

Noah: No, you aren't.

Dad: Yes, I am. I'm very good at it.

Noah: Well, I can't do that.

Dad: It's fun.

Noah: No, I'm bad at that.

Dad: You can't throw or catch a ball, you can't run fast. Look! Yoga!

Noah: No, Dad, I can't do yoga.

Dad: Why?

Noah: I'm bad at that!

Dad: Noah, exercise is good for you. You can't play football, you can't play trampoline basketball, you can't do hip-hop, and you can't do yoga. *What can you do?*

3. Listen and check the activity for Noah. 54

1 
☐

2 
☐

3 
☐

4. Listen and practice. 55

5. Read. Then write about yourself.

Hi! I'm Lydia. I'm very good at basketball. There are 12 players on my team. It's fun. I'm not very good at table tennis. I can't hit the ball! I'm bad at soccer. What about you?

____

____

____

____

____

6. Tell your classmates about your abilities.

I'm very good at soccer. What about you?

WORKBOOK, 135

BONUS Magazine

EXTREME SPORTS!

1. Answer the questions. Then talk to your classmate.

1. Are extreme sports interesting?
2. What extreme sports are your favorites?

2. Read the fact files about extreme sports.

Popular since the 1990s, extreme sports involve high speeds, dangerous heights, specialist technical skills, and specialized equipment. Extreme sports are popular among 15 to 35-year-olds.

IN THE WATER

These are water-based sports like scuba diving, windsurfing, kitesurfing, wakeboarding, surfing, whitewater kayaking, and rafting.

UP IN THE AIR

These extreme sports include bungee jumping, skydiving, BASE jumping, paragliding, and hang gliding.

WINTER SPORTS

Winter-based sports include skiing, snowboarding and snowmobiling.

CLIFF AND CAVE

Cliff and cave-based sports include rock climbing, ice climbing, caving, free diving, mountaineering, and cave diving.

ON WHEELS

These extreme sports include BMX, skateboarding, mountain biking, inline skating, rally car, and motocross.

THE X GAMES

The **X Games** are an annual extreme sports event, organized by the U.S. TV station ESPN. Participants can win gold, silver, and bronze medals along with prize money. Games are usually held in the USA. The first Summer X Games were held in 1995 in Newport, Rhode Island. The first Winter X Games were held in 1997 at Big Bear Lake, California. The Winter X Games are held in January or February and the summer games are usually held in August.

EXTREME SPORTS GREATS

ASHLEY FIOLEK

Nickname: Rude Pea
Country: the USA
Born: 1990
Sport: motocross

Ashley won the Women's Motocross Championship in 2008, 2009, 2011, and 2012. She retired in 2012. Ashley is profoundly deaf and she can't hear her bike.

SHAUN WHITE

Nickname: Flying Tomato
Country: the USA
Born: 1986
Sports: snowboarding and skateboarding

Shaun won 23 gold medals at the X Games and a perfect 100 in the men's Snowboard Superpipe. He competed in the Winter and Summer X Games.

FABIOLA DA SILVA

Nickname: Fabby
Country: Brazil
Born: 1979
Sport: vert skating

Da Silva, from São Paulo, Brazil, is the most successful female athlete in X Games history. She has seven gold medals.

3. How about you? Who is your favorite extreme sports star?

REVIEW 3

VOCABULARY

1. Label the picture.

~~kitchen~~	sofa	bed	dining room	bedroom
table	living room	fridge	TV	

2. Write the name of the sports.

1. We can run, catch the ball, and throw the ball into a hoop.
   basketball
2. We can kick the ball, but we can't catch the ball.
   ______
3. We can hit the ball over the net with a racket.
   ______
4. There is no racket, but we can hit the ball over a net.
   ______

3. Number the story conversation 1–6.

Cool! Let's play tennis. ☐

Are you good at baseball? 1

Really? How about tennis? ☐

Yes, I'm good at tennis. ☐

Great! I can play tennis too! ☐

No, I'm not good at baseball. ☐

GRAMMAR

4. Look at the picture. Then answer the questions.

1. Is there a knight in the castle?
   Yes, there is.
2. Are there windows in the tower?
   ______
3. Are there flags on the drawbridges?
   ______
4. Is there a bed in the kitchen?
   ______
5. Is there a moat?
   ______
6. Are there tables in the hall?
   ______

5. Read and answer the questions.

Martina is two years old. She can run and jump. She can throw a ball, but she can't catch or kick a ball. Renata is eight years old. She can kick, throw, and catch a ball. She can play volleyball, jump up, and hit the ball. She can play video games too, but she can't play basketball. Paul is 12 years old. He can play soccer, basketball, and volleyball. He's not good at table tennis.

1. Can Martina run and jump?
   Yes, she can.
2. Can Martina catch a ball?
   ______
3. Can Paul play basketball?
   ______
4. Can Martina and Renata throw a ball?
   ______

Circle.

1. Which unit was more interesting?
   Unit 5 (Home Sweet Home) / Unit 6 (Sports World!)
2. Which unit was more difficult?
   Unit 5 (Home Sweet Home) / Unit 6 (Sports World!)

PUZZLES, 104

UNIT 7

OUR DAYS

VOCABULARY

1. Listen and practice. 56

1 get up

2 eat breakfast

Good morning! I'm Hal. This is my bedroom. It's my brother's bedroom, too. Our mom says, (1) "Get up!" and we jump out of bed!

WAKE UP

129 likes

BREAKFAST

Hi. I'm Molly. I (2) ________________ in the kitchen. We eat healthy food every day. My mom and dad are nutritionists.

It's time to (3) ________________. My books are in my backpack. I can see my friends at school. That's my friend Kathy.

295 likes

Good evening. This is my family. We (7) ________________ together in the dining room. We talk and have fun.

DINNER

112 likes

In the evening, I play basketball in the yard. Then I (8) ________________ in the bathroom.

SHOWER

296 likes

GO TO BED

155 likes

It's 10 o'clock. It's time to (9) ________________. Good night!

go to school

eat lunch

come home

do homework

eat dinner

take a shower

go to bed

This is the school dining room. It's called the cafeteria. We (4) ____________ here. I can eat with my classmates. It's fun!

After school, I (5) ____________. That's my dog Fritz. "Hello! Fritz, you're a good dog!" Fritz can jump and catch a ball.

I (6) ____________ in the living room. I use my new laptop. It's great.

2. Read and write the words. Then listen and check. 57

3. Circle the correct option to complete the sentences.

1. I come home ...
   a. with a nutritionist.
   b. and play with my dog.

2. I do homework ...
   a. on my new laptop.
   b. in my bedroom.

3. I take a shower ...
   a. to get up in the morning.
   b. to keep clean.

4. I eat lunch ...
   a. in the cafeteria at school.
   b. in our dining room at home.

5. I go to school ...
   a. with my parents.
   b. with my books in a backpack.

4. How about you? Write the things you do every day. Talk to your classmate.

WORKBOOK, 136

GRAMMAR

1. Look at the sentences. Then read the examples in the *Grammar* box.

SIMPLE PRESENT

I You We They	**go** to school in the morning.	I You We They **don't go** to school in the afternoon.
Do I / you / we / they	go to school in the morning?	Yes, I (you/we/they) **do**. No, I (you/we/they) **don't**.

2. Look at the pictures. Use the phrases in parentheses to complete the sentences.

1. We _don't eat lunch_ at home. (eat lunch)
2. They ________________ in the evening. (do homework)
3. I ________________ in the morning. (take a shower)
4. They ________________ in their bedrooms. (eat dinner)

3. Look at the pictures in **Activity 2**. Answer the questions.

1. Do we eat lunch at school?
   Yes, we do.
2. Do they do homework in the morning?
   ____
3. Do you take a shower at school?
   ____
4. Do they eat dinner in the dining room?
   ____

READING

4. Match the words to the pictures.

1 
2 
3 

☐ flood
☐ boat
☐ library

5. Read and underline the words from **Activity 4**.

Hi! My name is Chandri. I'm 11 years old and I'm a student at a school in Bangladesh. My school is in a boat!

In Bangladesh, there is lots of water. There are floods, and students can't go to school. But there are lots of boats, and they are our schools. There are 100 boat schools in Bangladesh. My boat school is great!

I get up in the morning and I eat breakfast with my mother and my sister, Abida. Then we go to school in the boat. There are 25 students in my class, boys and girls. There is a laptop and there is Internet on the boat. There is a bookshelf and there are lots of books — it is a library!

School is in the morning, from 9 to 12. Then we come home. Abida and I have lunch and do homework in the afternoon. In the evening, we eat dinner and we go to bed.

6. Answer the questions. Use short answers.

1. Do Chandri and Abida go to school? Yes, they do.
2. Do they go to school with their mother? ______________________
3. Do Chandri and Abida eat breakfast? ______________________

7. Talk to a classmate. Compare your school to Chandri and Abida's school.

WORKBOOK, 137

CLIL ART

59 PRONUNCIATION

Pronunciation of "o'clock"
- one o'clock
- six o'clock
- three o'clock
- nine o'clock

TELLING THE TIME

GRAMMAR

1. Listen and practice. 58

one o'clock

two ten

three fifteen

four thirty

five forty-five

six fifty-five

LANGUAGE TIP

Twelve o'clock in the afternoon is **noon**. Twelve o'clock at night is **midnight**.
For times between 12:01 and 12:10, we say **twelve-o-**..., for example, twelve-o-five (not twelve five).

TELLING THE TIME

What time do	I you we they	get up?	I You We They	get up **at seven o'clock**.

2. Write the questions and answers.

1.

What time do you eat breakfast?
I eat breakfast at 7:10.

2.

What time ____________ ?
I go ____________ .

3.

____
____

4.

____
____

A DAY IN THE LIFE OF THE THEATER

3. Read and listen. 60

This is a beautiful old theater. There are plays and musicals at this theater. The theater is a busy place.

10:00 a.m. — 7:00 p.m.

We are the theater managers. We come to the theater at 10 in the morning. We talk to people all day. We open the doors at 6:00 p.m.

1:30 p.m. — 11:00 p.m.

We are the directors. The actors practice in the afternoon, and we help them.

7:00 p.m. — 11:00 p.m.

This is the orchestra. They play music for the play or musical. They come to the theater at 7:00.

7:00 p.m. — 10:45 p.m.

These people are in the audience. They sit down in the theater at 7:30 p.m. The show is from 8:00 p.m. to 10:30 p.m. It's great!

4. Who is at the theater at these times? Write.

theater managers
actors
audience
directors
orchestra

LANGUAGE TIP
The expression **a.m.** is used for the times in the morning, and **p.m.** is used for times in the afternoon and evening.

1. 10:00 a.m. *theater managers*
2. 3:00 p.m. ____________________
3. 7:15 p.m. ____________________

WORKBOOK, 138

COMMUNICATION

1. Listen and read. 61

2. What time is it? Check ✔ the correct word.

- time for lunch ☐
- time for soccer ☐
- time for bed ☐

3. Listen and practice. 62

4. Read. Then write about your routine.

Hi! I'm Fernanda. I'm a student in Belo Horizonte. I get up at 6:30 a.m. I have breakfast at 7:00 a.m. and I go to school at 7:15 a.m. I come home at 12:30 p.m. Time for lunch! I do my homework. We eat dinner at 7:30 p.m. I take a shower and then it's time for bed. I go to bed at 10:00 p.m.

5. Tell your classmates about your routine.

LANGUAGE TIP

You can say that it's **time** for lots of things. For example, you can say:
Time for dinner.
Time for bed.
Time for TV.

WORKBOOK, 139

BONUS Magazine

CLOCKS

1. **Answer the questions. Then talk to your classmate.**

1. How many clocks are there in your home?
2. Are the clocks interesting or special?

2. **Read the infographic about clocks.**

Telling the Time

Sundial
As the sun moves across the sky, a sundial can measure the length of a day.

Hourglass
As glass technology developed in the 14th century, it became possible to make hourglasses.

Water Clock
The design for this big water clock is 400 years old.

Blue Water Clock
This clock is in a shopping center. It tells the time with blue water.

Candle Clock
Marked candles were used for telling the time in China in the sixth century. They were also in use in England in the tenth century.

Plant Clock
This clock is a plant clock. It's in a park in Brazil.

Cool Clocks

Domino Clock
This is a fun clock. You tell the time with dominoes!

The Mystery Clock
You can't see the numbers for the minutes in this clock. We only see the hour.

Editoria de arte

Three Famous Clocks

Grand Central Station
This clock is in a train station in New York. There are four faces of it.

Big Ben
This clock is on a tower in London, England. Big Ben is the name of the bell in the tower.

The Prague Astronomical Clock
This beautiful old clock in the Czech Republic dates from the 15th century.

3. What are your three favorite clocks from the ones presented here?

1. ______________________________
2. ______________________________
3. ______________________________

4. Design a clock. Describe it. Then talk to your classmate about it.

UNIT 8 FAVORITE FOODS

VOCABULARY

1. Listen and practice. 63

1 bread

2 pasta

3 
ice cream

4 
rice

5 
eggs

6 
steak

7 
beans

8 
fish

9 
chicken

2. **Read and write the words.**

3. **Listen and check.** 64

4. **Write.**

1. What's this?
   It's ___steak___.

2. What's this?
   It's ______________.

3. What's this?
   It's ______________.

4. What's this?
   It's ______________.

5. What are these?
   They're ______________.

5. **Write your five favorite foods.**

WORKBOOK, 140

Editoria de arte

GRAMMAR

1. Look at the sentences. Then read the examples in the *Grammar* box.

Editoria de arte

SIMPLE PRESENT: HE, SHE, IT

I You We They	**like**	pasta.	I You We They	**don't like**	steak.
He She It	**likes**	salad.	He She It	**doesn't like**	fish.

2. Circle the correct alternative.

1. My father *like* / *likes* bread.
2. Anna *doesn't like* / *don't like* pizza.
3. Max *likes* / *like* steak.
4. Janice's grandmother *don't like* / *doesn't like* ice cream.
5. My dog *like* / *likes* chicken!
6. My friend is a cake decorator, but he *doesn't like* / *don't like* cake.

3. Read and write the correct form of the verbs in parentheses.

Dinner with my family is complicated! My mother (1) ___likes___ (like) salad, but my father (2) ____________ (not / like) it. He (3) ____________ (like) rice, beans, and steak. My sister (4) ____________ (like) pizza and French fries, but my mother and father (5) ____________ (not / like) unhealthy food. My brother (6) ____________ (like) pasta, but my sister (7) ____________ (not / like) it. I (8) ____________ (like) fish and bread. There is one thing we all (9) ____________ (like): ice cream!

READING

4. Look at the second picture in **Activity 5**. Then circle the correct alternative.

Jamie Oliver is a *game designer* / *chef* / *photographer*.

5. Read the review of a TV show.

My Favorite TV show:

Jamie Oliver's Food Revolution

Jamie Oliver is a British chef. He's a celebrity and his TV shows are very popular. Jamie likes food, but he really likes healthy food. He likes salad, for example. Salad is good for you, and it doesn't contain lots of extra salt and sugar. Jamie likes food you can make at home: eggs, rice, beans, chicken, and fish, for example.

Jamie doesn't like unhealthy food. What is unhealthy food? To Jamie, unhealthy food is "fast food": pizza, hamburgers, hot dogs, French fries, and ice cream. Students in British and American schools eat lunch at school, and Jamie doesn't like the food in those schools. There's a lot of fast food in British and American schools.

On Jamie's TV shows, he teaches students and their families to make healthy food. They're interesting TV shows, and now, I can make healthy food!

6. Read the review again and write **G** if it is good for you and **NG** if it is not good and you should only eat a little.

salt

salad

pizza

sugar

fish

French fries

rice

WORKBOOK, 141

CLIL GEOGRAPHY

LANGUAGE TIP
American English: **French fries**
British English: **chips**

GRAMMAR

1. Listen and practice. Then read the sentences from the *Grammar box.* 65

U.K.

fish and chips

China

noodles

Mexico

tacos

The USA

hamburgers

Japan

sushi

Italy

pizza

66 PRONUNCIATION

When you ask a **yes-no** question, your voice should go up at the end.
- **Is she your mother?** ↗
  Yes, she is. / No, she isn't.
- **Can you help me?** ↗
  Yes, I can. / No, I can't.
- **Does he want noodles?** ↗
  Yes, he does. / No, he doesn't.

When you ask questions with **wh-**words, your voice should go down at the end.
- **What time is it?** ↘
  It's…
- **How many caps are there?** ↘
  There are…

SIMPLE PRESENT QUESTIONS: *HE, SHE, IT*

	He She	**wants**	pizza.	He She	**doesn't want**	tacos.
Does	he she	**want**	pizza?	Yes, he **does**. / Yes, she **does**. No, he **doesn't**. / No, she **doesn't**.		

2. Look at the pictures and write.

1 

2 

3 

4 

1. Does she want noodles? No, she doesn't. She wants a hamburger.
2. Does he want pizza? ______________________
3. Does she want sushi? ______________________
4. Does he want tacos? ______________________
5. Does she want a hamburger? ______________________
6. Does she want fish and chips? ______________________

5 
6 

Foods from Around the World

3. Read and listen. Then circle *True* or *False*. 67

Tacos come from Mexico, but they are popular all over the world. You can get tacos in Mexican restaurants, or you can make tacos at home too.

Hamburgers are a popular fast food from the USA. You can also eat chicken burgers and cheeseburgers.

Pizza is a flat bread with tomato and cheese on it. Pizza originally comes from Naples, a city in Italy.

Fish and chips is a traditional food from the UK It's very popular. It's good, but it's not very healthy.

Sushi is made of rice with fish or vegetables, and it's a traditional food from Japan. There are many kinds of sushi. There are cheap and very expensive sushi restaurants.

Noodles are delicious. They're from China, and there are thick and thin noodles. They're a very old food — 4,000 years old!

Lots of foods are global. Immigrants leave their countries and take their favorite foods with them. For example, pizza is from Italy, but you can eat it in Brazil or Russia too. In Italy, pizza is thin and simple. In Chicago, in the USA, local pizza is thick. There's a lot of cheese!

Curry is very popular in India. Lots of immigrants from India live in the U.K. Curry is very popular there, but the Indians make the food in a different way for the people in the U.K.

1.	Hamburgers are a popular fast food.	True	False
2.	Fish and chips isn't a very healthy food.	True	False
3.	Sushi is made of bread with fish and vegetables.	True	False
4.	Noodles are an old food from China.	True	False

WORKBOOK, 142

COMMUNICATION

1. Look at the menu in **Activity 2**. Where is the food in the restaurant from?

a. China. **b.** Mexico. **c.** Italy.

LANGUAGE TIP

In the USA, people write cents or decimal numbers with a period, not a comma.
$1.99, not $1,99.

2. Listen and read. 68

Appetizers

Homemade bread	$4.99
Mozzarella sticks	$7.99
Garden salad	$3.99

Pasta

Lasagna	$12.99
Spaghetti with tomato sauce	$10.99
Fettuccine with meat sauce	$11.99

Dessert

Ice cream (chocolate or vanilla)	$4.99
Brownie with ice cream	$5.99
Cheesecake with strawberry sauce	$5.99

Drinks

Orange juice	$2.99
Iced tea	$1.99
Soft drink	$1.99

Server: Good evening! I'm Steve and I'm your server this evening.

Abby: Good evening. I'd like the spaghetti with tomato sauce.

Server: Spaghetti with tomato sauce. OK. Would you like an appetizer with that?

Abby: Yes, I'd like a garden salad, please.

Server: And to drink?

Abby: I'd like iced tea, please.

Server: So that's garden salad, spaghetti with tomato sauce, and orange juice.

Abby: No, not orange juice. Iced tea.

Server: I'm sorry. Iced tea.

Abby: Yes, thank you.

Server: And how about you, sir?

Mike: For my appetizer, I'd like a garden salad too.

Server: Garden salad.

Mike: Sorry, not the salad. I'd like mozzarella sticks.

Server: OK.

Mike: And lasagna.

Server: Mozzarella sticks and lasagna. Would you like something to drink?

Mike: Orange juice, please.

Server: OK!

Mike: Thank you.

3. Listen and circle what Abby and Mike choose for dessert. 69

1. Abby: a. cheesecake b. brownie with ice cream c. chocolate ice cream
2. Mike: a. cheesecake b. brownie with ice cream c. vanilla ice cream

4. Listen and practice. 70

5. Read. Then write about your family.

6. Tell your classmates about your family members.

WORKBOOK, 143

BONUS Magazine

Chocolate Brownies

1. Answer the questions. Then talk to a classmate.

1. Do you like brownies? ______________________
2. Can you make them? ______________________

2. Read. Then circle the ingredients in the recipe below.

This recipe for brownies is easy and yummy.

Ingredients

- 1 2/3 cup (335 g) sugar
- 3/4 cup (150 g) cocoa
- 1 1/3 cup (175 g) flour
- 1/2 teaspoon (2 g) baking powder
- 1/4 teaspoon (1 g) salt
- 2 eggs
- 2 tablespoons (30 ml) water
- 3/4 cup (150 g) butter or margarine (melted)
- 2 teaspoons (10 ml) vanilla

Editoria de arte

Directions

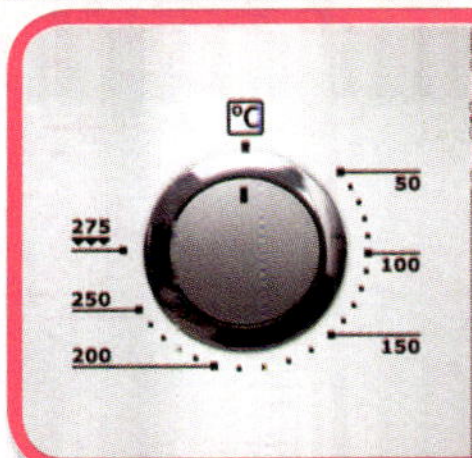

Step 1

Heat the oven to 180 °C.

Step 2

Grease a large baking pan.

Step 3

Mix the dry ingredients — flour, cccoa, baking powder, sugar, and salt — in a bowl.

Step 4

Add the wet ingredients — eggs, water, butter, and vanilla. Stir well.

Step 5

Put the mixture into the baking pan.

Step 6

Bake for 18 to 25 minutes. Test with a wooden toothpick.

Step 7

Enjoy the brownies!

Editoria de arte

3. **Number these steps 1–7.**

- [ ] Grease the baking pan.
- [ ] Eat the brownies.
- [ ] Mix the dry ingredients.
- [ ] Put the brownie mixture in the baking pan
- [ ] Bake the brownies for 18–25 minutes.
- [ ] Add the wet ingredients.
- [1] Heat the oven to 180 °C.

4. **Write a recipe. Then tell your classmate the steps.**

RECIPES

REVIEW 4

VOCABULARY

1. Write the words. Then match.

take do ~~eat~~ get

1. ___eat___ lunch [c]
2. ________ a shower [ ]
3. ________ homework [ ]
4. ________ up [ ]

2. Write the names of food on the menu.

1. ___rice___
2. ________
3. ________
4. ________
5. ________
6. ________
7. ________
8. ________
9. ________

3. Number the dialogue 1–9.

[ ] OK. Let's go to the Japanese restaurant then.
[ ] 12:30? It's time for lunch.
[1] What time is it?
[ ] Would you like Mexican or Japanese food?
[ ] Great! Let's go now.
[ ] It's 12:30.
[ ] I'd like sushi.
[ ] Let's go to a restaurant.

GRAMMAR

4. Look at the table. Write affirmative and negative sentences about your day.

IN THE MORNING	IN THE AFTERNOON	IN THE EVENING
1. get up	**3.** eat breakfast	**5.** do homework
2. eat dinner	**4.** come home	**6.** eat lunch

1. I get up in the morning.
2. ______
3. ______
4. ______
5. ______
6. ______

5. Unscramble the questions. Then write your answers.

1. up / get / do / time / you / what / ?
   What time do you get up?
   ______
   I get up at ______.
2. go / time / you / what / do / school / to / ?
   ______
   ______
   I go to school at ______.
3. time / what / eat / do / lunch / you / ?
   ______
   ______
   I eat lunch at ______.
4. do / go / time / to / bed / you / what / ?
   ______
   ______
   I go to bed at ______.

Circle.

1. Which unit was more interesting?
   Unit 7 (Our Days) / Unit 8 (Favorite Foods)
2. Which unit was more difficult?
   Unit 7 (Our Days) / Unit 8 (Favorite Foods)

PUZZLES, 104 BOARD GAME, 108

PROJECT 1

FAMOUS *families*

1. Who are the people in the picture below? Talk to your teacher and classmates about them.

Editoria de arte

2. Complete the text using the words below.

daughter | 's | sons | soccer player | singer

This is David and Victoria Beckham ____ family. This is a famous family because David is a former ____________ and Victoria is a pop ____________, originally from the group the Spice Girls. They have three ____________ and one ____________.

3. Is your family big too? Talk to a classmate about your family.

4. Refer to the text about the Beckhams. Write about another famous family. Choose a family you know or refer to the one in the picture below. You can draw or stick a picture, or even record a video talking about them.

5. Share your text and/or video with your classmates.

PROJECT 2

Dream Home

1. Are any of these your dream home? Talk to your teacher and classmates about them.

a 

b 

c 

d 

The house in picture C is a dream home for me. It's modern and pretty. I love its windows.

Editoria de arte

2. Plan your dream home. You can use an app or create a scale model.

3. Share your dream home with your classmates.

PUZZLES 1 UNITS 1–4

Cool Jobs

Find seven jobs in the word search.

M	S	A	S	T	R	O	N	O	M	E	R	V	M	C
Y	A	S	G	W	C	K	O	J	V	T	L	K	X	A
V	C	R	P	A	Y	K	F	D	F	M	N	P	R	K
Q	Y	P	I	T	M	K	E	G	M	C	N	O	B	E
X	V	U	U	N	K	E	O	C	W	H	I	V	T	D
Z	O	Q	I	N	E	I	D	U	E	Y	S	O	I	E
Q	A	C	T	O	R	B	T	E	W	K	E	Y	W	C
R	U	I	O	N	W	C	I	O	S	O	K	V	F	O
Y	A	B	U	M	J	X	M	O	G	I	F	T	G	R
U	P	E	R	W	Q	N	I	O	L	E	G	Y	W	A
I	N	N	G	D	V	Z	N	I	A	O	K	N	W	T
K	X	I	U	A	V	A	F	J	B	S	G	S	E	O
K	U	R	I	R	W	M	T	C	A	C	B	I	B	R
M	B	X	D	G	M	H	P	W	D	D	B	Z	S	F
G	C	M	E	T	E	O	R	O	L	O	G	I	S	T

Code Breaker

Break the code and find out what the secret message is. Then answer the question.

A	B	C	D	E	F	G	H	I	J	K	L	M
Њ	Л	Ф	Ж	Й	Ю	д	Ш	Ъ	Ы	з	ɜ	Ю

N	O	P	Q	R	S	T	U	V	W	X	Y	Z
Ц	Ϙ	ς	ғ	ɗ	щ	ɘ	ϖ	Э	Ђ	Ѓ	ӡ	φ

ЂШϘ Ъщ ӡϘϖɗ ЮЊЭϘɗЪɘЙ щЪЦдЙɗ?

SENTENCE GENERATOR

Make up sentences using the words.
How many sentences can you create?

like | Nice | veterinarian. | I'd | How | grandmother | are | geologist.

My | socks? | a | much | Those | you. | backpacks | ones, | the | I'm

yellow | are | meet | is | not | the | a | please. | heavy. | to

SPELLING BEE

Look at the pictures and spell the words with your classmates. The one who spells the most words correctly is the winner.

PAGE 11

PAGE 11

PAGE 24

PAGE 24

PAGE 33

PAGE 33

PAGE 43

PAGE 43

S–I–N–G–E–R

Good!

PUZZLES 2 UNITS 5–8

FURNITURE CROSSWORD

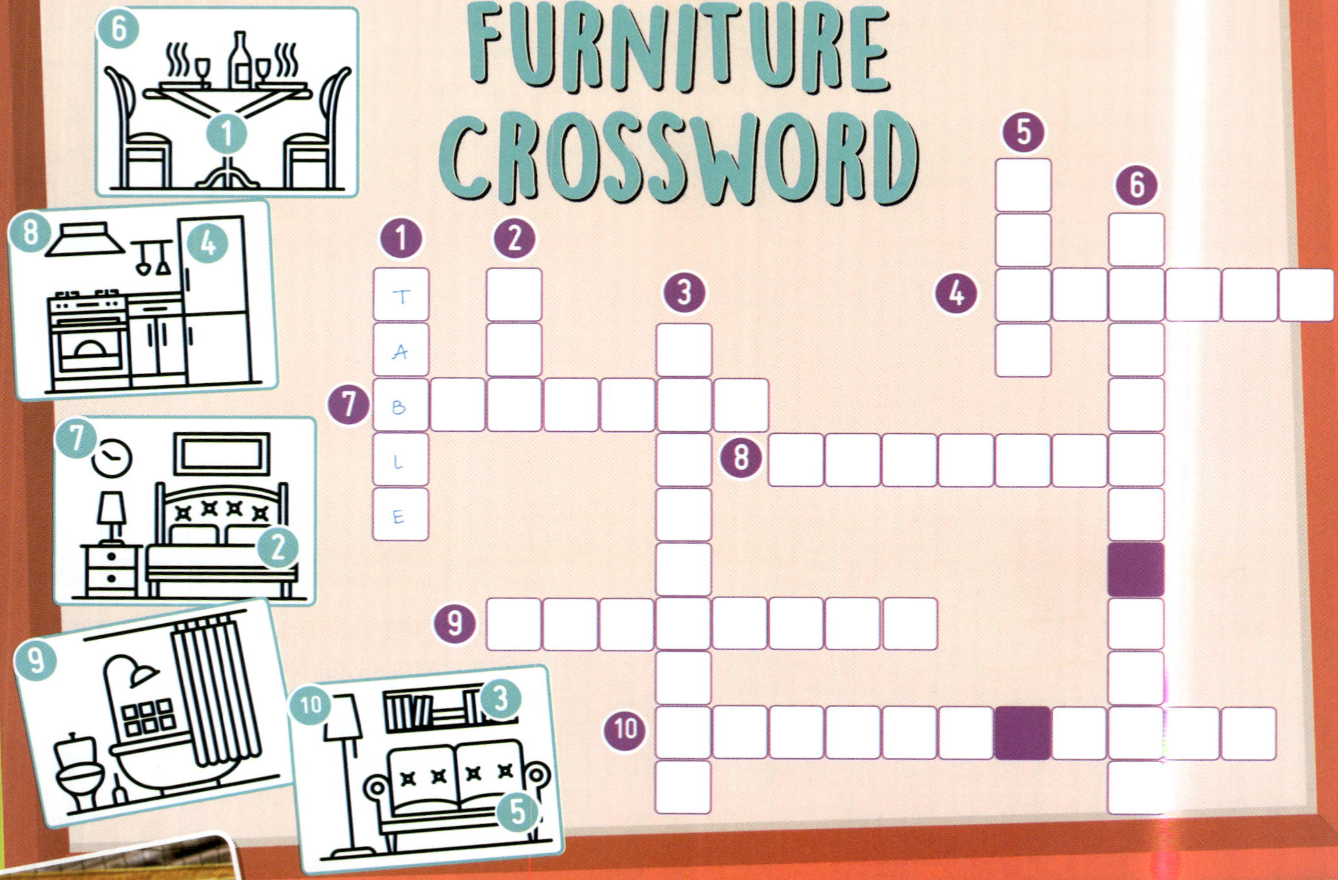

CODE BREAKER

Use the code to write Paula's list. Then check the things you do.

A	C	D	E	F	G	H	I	K	L	N	O	P	R	S	T	U	V	W	X
T	S	R	Q	P	O	N	M	L	K	J	I	H	G	F	E	D	C	B	A

☐ OQE QJIDON FKQQH GET ENOUGH SLEEP

☐ NTCQ PDJ ____________

☐ RGMJL BTEQG ____________

☐ LQQH SKQTJ ____________

☐ QTE OIIR PIIR ____________

☐ QAQGSMFQ ____________

Color coded sentence

Use the words with the same color. Put the words in the correct order to make sentences.
Then write the times you do the things.

I	go	at	take	I	I	at	I	get
bed	at	come	go	at	lunch	shower	school	at
eat	a	I	I	home	at	to	up	to

1. I get up at 7:15 .
2. ______________________ .
3. ______________________ .
4. ______________________ .
5. ______________________ .
6. ______________________ .

Food Wordsearch

Look at the pictures. Circle the words in the puzzle.

T	H	A	M	B	U	R	G	E	R	A	P	B	M
K	E	V	S	F	T	X	E	B	N	Y	T	R	A
S	U	S	H	I	A	W	A	T	S	T	U	E	Y
P	D	O	G	S	Z	I	C	E	C	R	E	A	M
A	Q	E	Y	H	E	N	T	N	E	H	E	D	R
S	A	O	D	F	G	O	C	H	I	C	K	E	N
T	H	T	S	O	G	D	R	T	R	K	B	H	E
A	A	V	D	E	S	F	O	I	S	T	E	A	K

BOARD GAME 1
CASTLE
jac et / expe sive / It's an / black /.
You are your father's....
START
$25
Spell
Your... is your uncle's son
Say: 34
What are they?
START
Your... is your mother's daughter.
What are they?
Say: 58
a / beautiful / That's / cap / orange /.
YOU

LUDO

• HOW TO PLAY •

You need: dice / counters

How to play: Choose a color to start. Each player rolls the dice and goes all the way around the board. Then the player goes in towards the castle in the center. If one of the players can't answer the questions in each square, he /she misses a turn!

The first one to get to the castle is the winner.

BOARD GAME 2

AMAZING

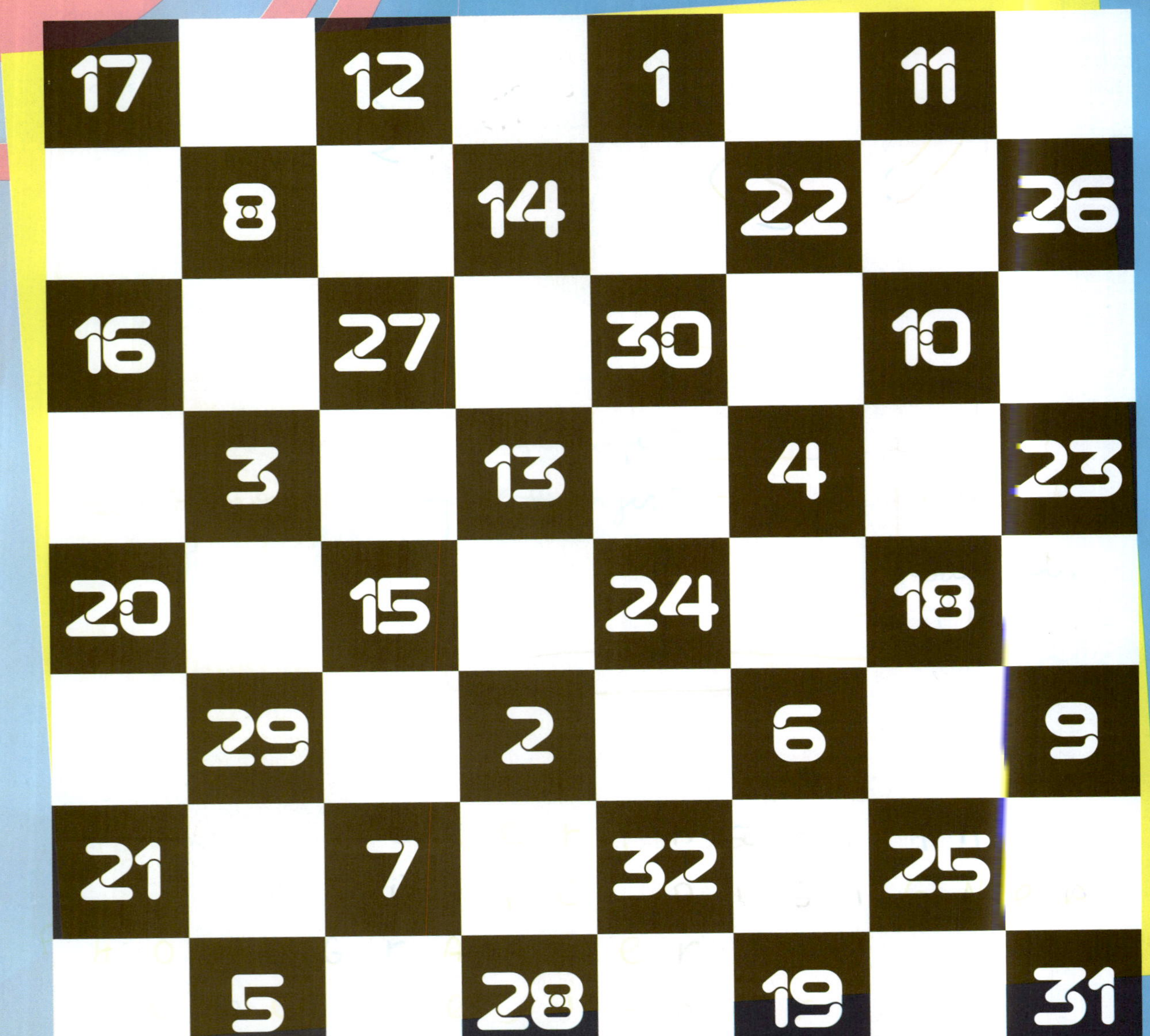

CHECKERS

6. This is a ...
7. Is there a table in the dining room?
8. Are there two beds in this bedroom?
9. Is there a tower in this castle?
10. Basketball players can / can't kick the ball.
11. Volleyball players can / can't hit the ball.
12. You can / can't throw the ball in baseball, but not in table tennis.
13. We ... at 7:10.
14. I ... at 8:05.
15. He ... at 2:30.
16. She ... at 9:00.
17. He ... at 7:30.
18. It's ...
12:00
19. It's ...
05:30
20. It's ...
03:10
21. It's ...
07:45
22. It's ...
03:30
23. What is this? It's ...
24. What is this? It's ...
25. What is this? It's ...
26. What is this? It's ...
27. What is this? It's ...
28. What is this? It's ...
29. What is this? It's ...
30. I like / don't like ...
31. I like / don't like ...
32. I like / don't like ...

GLOSSARY

[adj] = **adjective** – adjetivo
[n] = **noun** – substantivo
[v] = **verb** – verbo

A

actor • [n] ator, atriz
advertisement • [n] propaganda, anúncio
allowance • [n] mesada
aunt • [n] tia
awesome • [adj] incrível, impressionante

B

backpack • [n] mochila
bathroom • [n] banheiro
bean • [n] feijão
bed • [n] cama
bedroom • [n] quarto
big • [adj] grande
bookshelf • [n] prateleira
bread • [n] pão
breakfast • [n] café da manhã
brother • [n] irmão

C

cake • [n] bolo

cake

cap • [n] boné
caretaker • [n] cuidador
castle • [n] castelo
catch • [v] pegar, agarrar
cell phone • [n] telefone celular
century • [n] século
chairman • [n] presidente (de empresa)
chicken • [n] frango
come • [v] vir
cousin • [n] primo, prima

D

daughter • [n] filha
dining room • [n] sala de jantar
dinner • [n] jantar
do • [v] fazer
door • [n] porta
drawbridge • [n] ponte levadiça
dream • [n] sonho
dress • [n] vestido
drink • [v] beber
duchess • [n] duquesa

door

E

earthquake • [n] terremoto
eat • [v] comer
egg • [n] ovo
empire • [n] império
enjoyable • [adj] agradável
enough • [adj] suficiente, o bastante

F

father • [n] pai
fish • [n] peixe

fish

flag • [n] bandeira
flat • [adj] plano
flight • [n] voo
franchise • [n] franquia
fridge • [n] geladeira
furniture • [n] móveis

G

get up • [v] levantar(-se)
go • [v] ir
grandfather • [n] avô
grandmother • [n] avó

H

hall • [n] salão
have fun • [v] divertir-se
healthy • [adj] saudável
heavy • [adj] pesado
hit • [v] rebater, bater
home • [n] lar, casa
homemade • [adj] caseiro
homework • [n] lição de casa
hug • [v] abraçar
husband • [n] marido

I

ice cream • [n] sorvete

ice cream

ID card • [n] carteira de identificação

J

joy • [n] alegria

K

keep clean • [v] manter(-se) limpo
key • [n] chave
kick • [v] chutar
kitchen • [n] cozinha
knight • [n] cavaleiro

L

laptop • [n] computador portátil
light • [adj] leve; [n] luz
living room • [n] sala de estar
lunch • [n] almoço

M

manager • [n] gerente
memorabilia • [n] recordações
moat • [n] fosso
mother • [n] mãe

N

new • [adj] novo
notebook • [n] caderno

O

old • [adj] velho, antigo
owner • [n] dono

P

parents • [n] pais
pasta • [n] massa

pasta

pencil case • [n] estojo
prize • [n] prêmio

R

reef • [n] recife
reliable • [adj] confiável
research • [v] pesquisar; [n] pesquisa
rice • [n] arroz
run • [v] correr

S

sauce • [n] molho
shirt • [n] camisa
shoe • [n] sapato
short • [adj] curto
shower • [n] banho
singer • [n] cantor
sister • [n] irmã
skill • [n] habilidade
skirt • [n] saia
small • [adj] pequeno
soccer • [n] futebol
sock • [n] meia
son • [n] filho
spend • [v] gastar
steak • [n] bife

steak

strength • [n] força, resistência
supplier • [n] fornecedor
sweatshirt • [n] moletom

T

table tennis • [n] tênis de mesa, pingue-pongue
take • [v] tomar, pegar
taster • [n] provador, degustador
thick • [adj] grosso
thin • [adj] fino, magro
throw • [v] arremessar
tour guide • [n] guia turístico
tower • [n] torre
T-shirt • [n] camiseta

U

uncle • [n] tio

W

wall • [n] parede
wallet • [n] carteira
water • [n] água
waterslide • [n] toboágua
wedding • [n] casamento
wife • [n] esposa
window • [n] janela

window

wing • [n] asa
wish • [n] desejo; [v] desejar, querer

Y

yard • [n] jardim, quintal

WORKBOOK

UNIT 1

LESSON 1

1. Write *a* or *an*.

1. ____ singer
2. ____ graphic designer
3. ____ nutritionist
4. ____ actor
5. ____ cake decorator
6. ____ veterinarian
7. ____ game designer
8. ____ photographer
9. ____ architect
10. ____ tour guide

2. Do the puzzle. Write the missing word.

Hello! I'm Mariah Davis and he's Oliver Walker. We're ________.

1 

2 

3 

4 

5 

6 

7 

8 

9 

LESSON 2

1. Choose the correct option.

1. You *is* / *are* a singer.
2. Alicia *is* / *are* a tour guide.
3. Julian and I *am* / *are* veterinarians.
4. I *am* / *are* an actor.
5. They *is* / *are* game designers.
6. Jason *am* / *is* an architect.

2. Complete the sentences with the words in the box.

She's	They're	singers	an	a	I'm

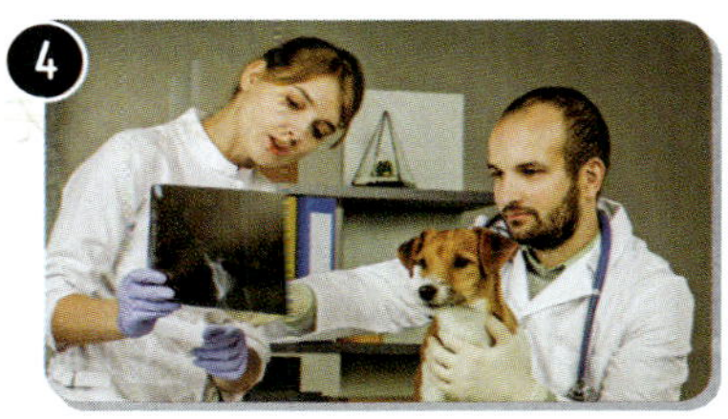

1. She's a graphic designer.
2. We're singers.
3. She's a photographer.
4. They're veterinarians.
5. I'm a cake decorator.
6. You're an architect.

3. Find the mistakes. Rewrite the sentences.

1. She are a tour guide. She is a tour guide.
2. They is students. They are students.
3. We's nutritionists. We're nutritionists.
4. Oliver's a actor. Oliver're a actor.
5. I am a game designer. I am an game designer.
6. Diego's a photographers. Diego're a photographers.
7. I are a cake decorator. I'm a cake decorator.

LESSON 3

1. Find six jobs in the word snake. Then write the words.

1. meteorologist
2. __________
3. __________
4. __________
5. __________
6. __________

2. Look at the chart. Write *is*, *isn't*, *are*, or *aren't*.

SARAH		✔				
MAX AND ALANA				✔		
ANTONIO					✔	
LILY AND KAYLEE			✔			
JACOB						✔
BIANCA	✔					

1. Sarah isn't a zoologist.
2. Max and Alana __________ geologists.
3. Antonio __________ an astronomer.
4. Lily and Kaylee __________ meteorologists.
5. Jacob __________ a botanist.
6. Bianca __________ a zoologist

LESSON 4

1. Complete the conversations with the words in the box.

OK	great	~~How~~	~~fine~~	~~you~~

1. How are __you__?
   I'm __fine__!
2. __How__ are you?
   I'm __great__.
3. I'm __OK__.

2. Read.

3. Who said it? Write *Steven Andrews*, *singer*, or *singers*.

1. "How are you, Robbie?" __Steven Andrews__
2. "We're fine, Steven." ______
3. "I'm not an actor." ______
4. "Good evening, singers!" ______
5. "I'm OK!" ______
6. "She's great!" ______

WORKBOOK

UNIT 2

LESSON 1

1. Find nine family members in the word search.

V A H D L U C C V H G E E C U S R E

G E C O U S I N S X R D C H A A S G

R T J I W O T T S M O T H E R O U C

A M F O D E H Y X C E E B T N C F S

N E I A U T B W M T B H E E T E A R

D V W U S G R A N D F A T H E R T I

M A R N B P O I Z T A P I Y M N H W

O U O T M K T S N E Y N E S Z E E R

T V E I V L H E X G K P A T W T R U

H N C Q E V E W Q R G O V U N C L E

E H N D Z A R A S I S T E R U A G S

R E I F H E S I N M U M O R C T L E

2. Use the words from **Activity 1** to write sentences about your family.

LESSON 2

1. Complete the chart.

Subject pronouns	Possessive adjectives
I	my
	your
he	
she	
	our
they	

2. Write the correct possessive adjective.

1 

Alyssa is ___her___ sister. (his / her)

4 

He's ___their___ father. (her / their)

2 

Robert is ___my___ brother. (my / their)

5 

They're ___our___ mother and father. (our / their)

3 

Russell and Stephanie are ___his___ uncle and aunt. (his / their)

6 

Who's she? Is she ___your___ cousin? (your / her)

LESSON 3

1. **Look at Amber's family tree. Do the puzzle.**

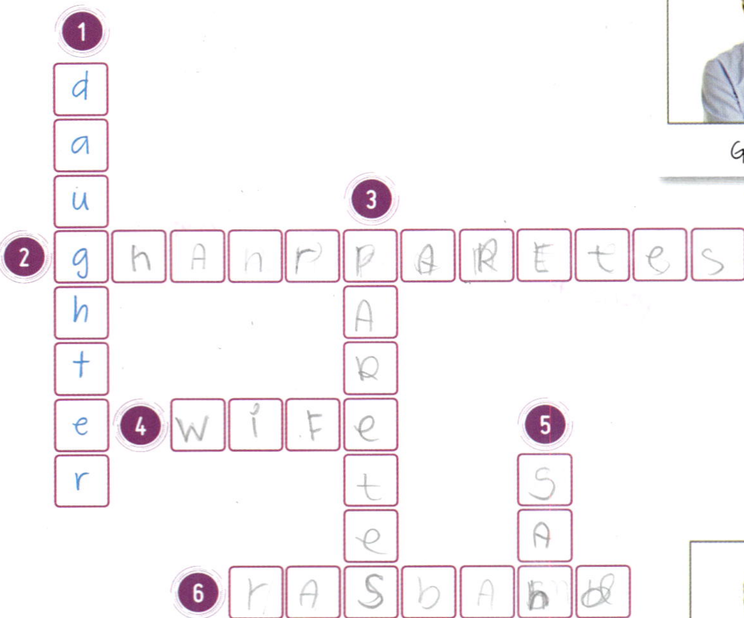

1. Amber is Steve and Allison's ....
2. George and Nancy are Amber's ....
3. Steve and Allison are Amber's ....
4. Allison is Steve's ....
5. Bruno is Steve and Allison's ....
6. George is Nancy's ....

2. **Answer the questions.**

1. Are George and Nancy Steve's parents? Yes, they are.
2. Is Amber Steve's sister? ______
3. Are Bruno and Sam Amber's brothers? ______
4. Are Steve and Allison Bruno's cousins? ______
5. Is Nancy Bruno's grandmother? ______
6. Is Steve Sam's father? ______
7. Is Amber George's daughter? ______

LESSON 4

1. Look at the people below. What are their jobs?

1. Angelina Jolie and Brad Pitt
   a. singers b. actors c. paramedics
2. Beyoncé and Jay Z
   a. models b. doctors c. singers

Angelina Jolie and Brad Pitt are actors. Angelina's parents are actors too. Their names are Jon Voight and Marcheline Bertrand. Brad's parents, William Alvin Pitt and Jane Etta, aren't actors. Angelina and Brad aren't married now. Their six children are Maddox, Zahara, Shiloh, Pax, Knox, and Vivienne.

Beyoncé and Jay Z are singers. Beyoncé's sister Solange Knowles is a singer too. Their parents aren't singers. Jay Z's mother is Gloria Carter. Beyoncé's parents are Célestine Knowles and Mathew Knowles. Beyoncé and Jay Z are parents—their oldest daughter is Blue Ivy Carter. They have twins too.

2. Read again. Then circle *True* or *False*.

1.	Brad Pitt is an actor.	True	False
2.	Jon Voight is a singer.	True	False
3.	Angelina Jolie and Brad Pitt are parents.	True	False
4.	Jay Z is a singer.	True	False
5.	Beyoncé's mother is Gloria Carter.	True	False
6.	Blue Ivy Carter is Célestine's daughter.	True	False

3. Circle the correct option.

1. Marcheline Bertrand is Angelina Jolie's *sister* / *mother* / *daughter*.
2. William Alvin Pitt and Jane Etta are Maddox's *parents* / *sons* / *grandparents*.
3. Vivienne is Angelina and Brad's *daughter* / *mother* / *sister*.
4. Jay Z is Beyoncé's *son* / *father* / *husband*.
5. Célestine Knowles is Solange's *daughter* / *mother* / *grandmother*.
6. Blue Ivy Carter is Gloria Carter's *daughter* / *sister*/ *granddaughter*.

WORKBOOK

UNIT 3

LESSON 1

1. Unscramble the letters. Write the name of the objects.

1. ksye keys
2. elpnic acse ______
3. bonekoto ______
4. lcle hnpoe ______
5. evdio mgea ______
6. DI dcra ______
7. tlaetb ______
8. cckkbaap ______
9. ploatp ______
10. wtalel ______

2. Complete the puzzle with words from **Activity 1**. What's in Jaden's backpack?

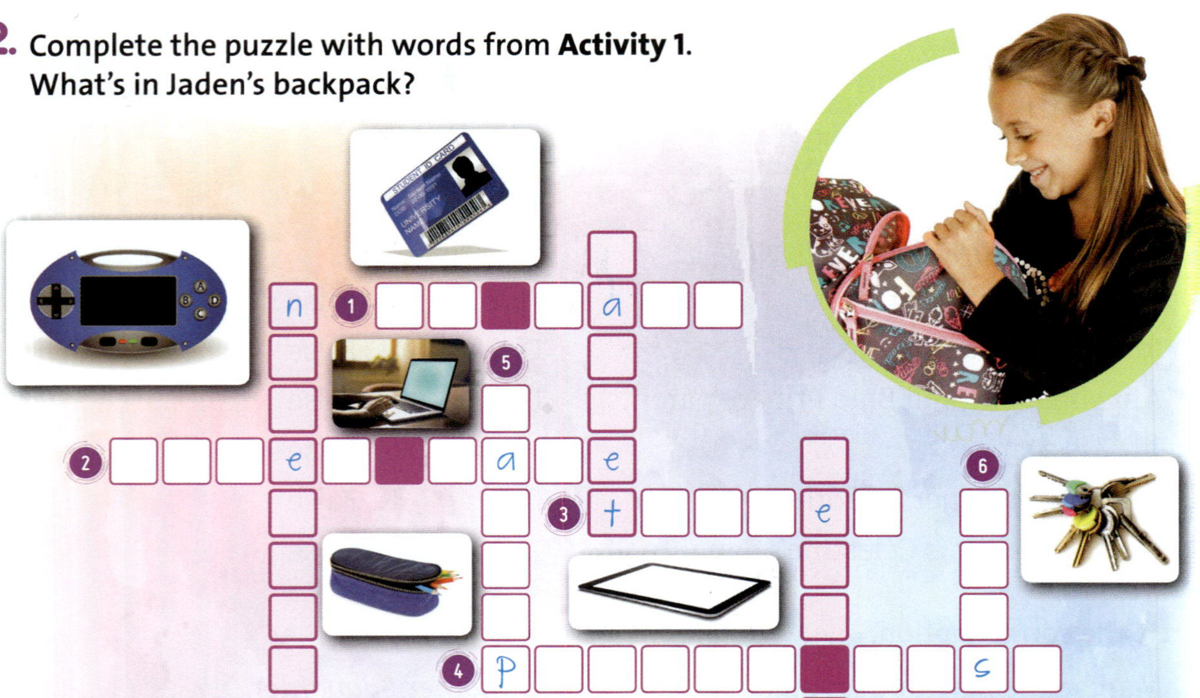

What is it?

______

______

______

LESSON 2

1. Circle the correct words to form questions and answers.

	What	is / are	it? / they?	They're / It's a	cell phone. / cell phones.
	What	are / is	it? / they?	It's a / They're	notebooks. / notebook.
	What	is / are	they? / it?	It's an / They're	ID card. / ID cards.
	What	are / is	they? / it?	They're / It's a	key. / keys.
	What	is / are	it? / they?	They're / It's a	video game. / video games.
	What	are / is	they? / it?	It's a / They're	laptops. / laptop.
	What	is / are	they? / it?	It's a / They're	wallet. / wallets.

2. Find the mistakes. Then rewrite the sentences.

1. What ~~are~~ it? It's a cell phone. What is it? It's a cell phone.
2. What is they? They're pencil cases. ______
3. What is it? It's a tablets. ______
4. What is it? It's laptops. ______
5. What are they? They're a backpacks. ______

LESSON 3

1. Circle the correct word.

1. *This* / *These* is my backpack.
2. *This* / *That* is my sister's video game.
3. *This* / *These* are my mother and father's cell phones.
4. *This* / *That* is my tablet.
5. *These* / *Those* are our pencil cases.
6. *This* / *That* isn't my ID card.
7. *This* / *That* is my ID card.

2. Match the words to the pictures.

1. new	3. light	5. big	7. long	9. thin
2. old	4. heavy	6. small	8. short	10. thick

1
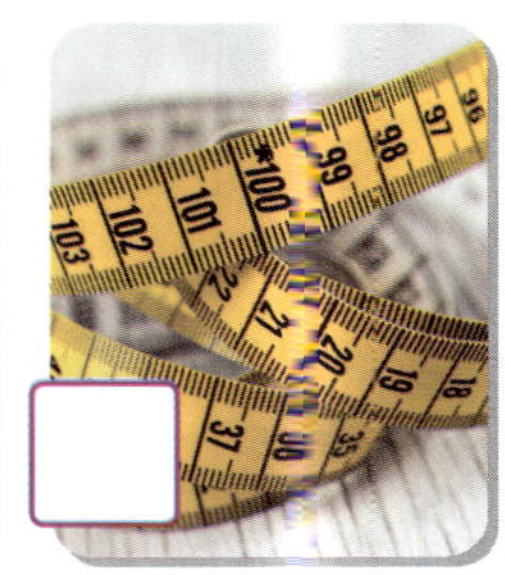

3. Use the adjectives from **Activity 2** to write about your things.

1. My backpack is heavy.
2. My keys are small.
3. My ____________________
4. My ____________________
5. My ____________________
6. My ____________________

LESSON 4

1. Look at the pictures. Which backpack is your favorite?

1

This is for students in the 1920s. It's very old, but is it a backpack?

2

This is a backpack now. Your backpack is probably similar. It's convenient, and it's good for school, but it's heavy with books in it.

3

These backpacks are for school too. One is a sling backpack and the other is a messenger bag. What's your opinion? Are they good for school?

4

This backpack isn't for students. It's big and heavy.

5

This is a backpack in the future. Your tablet, your laptop, and your books are in it. Is it good for school?

2. Look at **Activity 1**. Then write the numbers 1–5.

1. It's similar to my backpack. [2]
2. It's big and heavy. [ ]
3. They're for school, too. [ ]
4. This backpack is for the future. [ ]
5. It's old, and it isn't a backpack. [ ]

3. Write your opinion about the backpacks. Use the words below.

awesome

OK

funny

crazy

not OK

Backpack 1: This backpack is funny.

Backpack 2: This ______________________.

Backpacks 3: These ______________________.

Backpack 4: This ______________________.

Backpack 5: This ______________________.

WORKBOOK

UNIT 4

LESSON 1

1. Unscramble the words and write the name of the clothes.

1. o s s k c ___socks___
2. s h s t w i t e r a ________
3. r d s e s ________
4. o e h s s ________
5. s i r T h t ________
6. a p c ________
7. t r i s h ________
8. t c k j e a ________
9. k s t r i ________
10. a e n s j ________

2. Label the clothes using words from **Activity 1**. There is one extra word.

3. What's your opinion? Write sentences using the words in the box and the clothes in **Activity 1**.

beautiful	cheap	ugly	cool	~~expensive~~

1. The jacket is expensive.
2. ________
3. ________
4. ________
5. ________

LESSON 2

1. **Use words from the box to complete the descriptions.**

yellow   short   big   small   blue   ~~long~~   gray

1. Jade: a long white dress
2. Ronald: big ________ shoes
3. Skylar: a short ________ skirt
4. Jade: ________ green socks
5. Ronald: a ________ white shirt
6. Skylar: a big ________ cap
7. Jade: a ________ red sweatshirt

2. **Read the descriptions. Complete the sentences using the words in parentheses.**

1. Look! It's Ronald. He's awesome! It's a (1) small white (*white / small*) shirt and (2) ________ (*short / blue*) jeans. It's an awesome (3) ________ (*long / brown*) jacket too.
2. Wow! It's Jade. She's great! It's a (4) ________ (*red / big*) sweatshirt and a (5) ________ (*long / white*) dress. They're (6) ________ (*black / beautiful*) shoes. Awesome!
3. Oh, Skylar's beautiful! Look. It's a (7) ________ (*blue / big*) cap and a (8) ________ (*short / orange*) jacket. And her shoes! They're yellow. Beautiful!

LESSON 3

1. Write the numbers.

1. forty-seven 47
2. sixty-one ______
3. one hundred ______
4. twenty-four ______
5. fifty-nine ______
6. thirty-six ______
7. twelve ______
8. eighty ______
9. seventy-three ______
10. ninety-two ______
11. forty-eight ______
12. eighty-five ______

2. Write the words.

1. 99 ninety-nine
2. 23 ______
3. 39 ______
4. 81 ______
5. 37 ______
6. 50 ______
7. 28 ______
8. 92 ______
9. 46 ______
10. 64 ______

3. Write *is* or *are*. Then do the math and write the answers.

1. How much are the shoes? Twenty-two + twelve = ______ dollars
2. How much ______ the dress? Sixty-four + thirty-one = ______ dollars
3. How much ______ the jacket? Eleven + forty-seven = ______ dollars
4. How much ______ the jeans? Thirteen + thirty = ______ dollars
5. How much ______ the skirt? Thirty-two + nineteen = ______ dollars
6. How much ______ the T-shirts? Forty-seven + forty-six = ______ dollars

LESSON 4

1. Look at the pictures. Then read.

1 Leggings are a type of pants. They're good for school, sports, work, and leisure. And they're good for boys and girls!

Século XVI. Coleção particular.

2 Leggings are very old. The first leggings in art are from 1350.

3 Some leggings are two colors. These are gray and white.

Rigaud Hyacinthe. 1701. Óleo sobre tela. Louvre, Paris.

4 This is King Louis XIV of France. His leggings are white. Look at his shoes too.

5 Leggings are popular in movies. This is Audrey Hepburn in 1957.

6 These are Olivia Newton-John and John Travolta in the movie *Grease*, from 1978.

7 Leggings are good for singers too. This is Nicki Minaj in 2011. Her leggings are black, pink, orange, yellow, red, and green!

8 9 Are you a superhero? Where are your leggings?

10 11 Leggings are good for sports!

12 13 Leggings for men are sometimes called "meggings"! And leggings that are blue jeans are called "jeggings."

2. What's your opinion? Answer the questions and write the numbers.

1. Which leggings are ugly? The ones in picture 10.
2. Which leggings are beautiful? ____________
3. Which leggings are funny? ____________
4. Which leggings are crazy? ____________
5. Which leggings are expensive? ____________
6. Which leggings are your favorite? ____________

WORKBOOK

UNIT 5

LESSON 1

1. Circle furniture and rooms in the puzzle. Then write the words.

B	I	R	F	R	I	D	G	E	M	O	V	M	P	E	X	I
A	T	U	O	E	V	A	H	T	N	O	Z	I	B	A	J	E
T	H	B	O	O	K	S	H	E	L	F	U	T	E	T	I	S
H	I	E	S	B	I	U	S	A	E	D	I	R	D	B	U	P
R	O	D	N	E	T	D	D	I	N	I	N	G	R	O	O	M
O	H	T	K	D	C	Q	W	N	R	E	P	E	O	Z	A	F
O	S	O	F	A	H	S	T	A	B	L	E	H	O	S	R	Y
M	O	U	L	W	E	D	H	Y	C	M	E	T	M	L	T	A
H	A	S	T	E	N	K	S	A	K	V	T	O	E	Q	S	R
L	I	V	I	N	G	R	O	O	M	A	V	N	M	Y	O	D

FURNITURE	ROOMS
FRIDGE	B
S	K
B	Y
B	B
T	D
T	L

2. What are your three favorite rooms in your house?

____

____

LESSON 2

1. Look at the pictures in **Activity 2**. Check ✔ the things you see.

kitchen	☐	dining room	☐	TV	☐
bedroom	☐	living room	☐	chair	☐
bathroom	☐	sofa	☐	bookshelf	☐

2. Read and circle the correct alternatives.

Hi! My name is Erica and this is my family's RV. What is an RV? It's a recreational vehicle, and our house in July and August when there is no school. The RV is a big car, but a very small house! There (1) *is / are* two chairs for my parents and there (2) *is / are* a sofa too. There (3) *is / are* a small kitchen with a fridge. There (4) *is / are* a table in the dining room, and there (5) *is / are* three chairs at the table. There (6) *is / are* a very small bathroom. There (7) *is / are* a bedroom with a big bed for my grandparents. (8) *Is / Are* there a bed for me? Yes, there (9) *is / are*. It's the sofa.

3. Read the text again. Then write **T** (true) or **F** (false).

1. An RV is a big house. ☐ F
2. There are two chairs for Erica's parents. ☐
3. There's a small kitchen in the RV. ☐
4. The bathroom in the RV is big. ☐
5. There's a small bed in the bedroom. ☐
6. The sofa is Erica's bed. ☐

LESSON 3

1. **Unscramble and write the words.**

1. r o t w e tower
2. g a l f
3. a l w l
4. b r d w d r i e a g
5. o d r o
6. h l a l
7. g h k n t i
8. w n w i d o
9. a e s l c t
10. o a m t

2. **Look, count, and answer the questions.**

1. How many doors are there? There are two doors.
2. How many drawbridges are there?
3. How many knights are there?
4. How many moats are there?
5. How many flags are there?
6. How many windows are there?

LESSON 4

1. Look at the pictures. Then read the text. Which tree house is your favorite?

This is a great tree house. It's in a big tree with beautiful green leaves. It's small and gray. There's a small window, but where is the door?

This tree house is big. It's brown, and there is a big door. There are two windows in it. Is there a bed in the tree house? Is there a kitchen or a living room?

This is a red and white tree house and it's really cool. There's a door and two windows, but there aren't chairs, tables, or sofas.

This tree house is inside a bedroom, not in the yard. It's a bed too! It's yellow, green, orange, and white. There's are two windows in the tree house, and two windows in the bedroom. It's beautiful.

2. Complete the sentences with words from the box.

door	gray	one	~~big~~	windows	yard

1. Tree house 2 is brown and there's a ___big___ door.
2. There are two ____________ in tree houses 2, 3, and 4.
3. There is ____________ window in tree house 1.
4. Tree house 1 is ____________.
5. Tree house 4 isn't in a ____________. It's in a bedroom.
6. There's a ____________ and two windows in tree house 3.

WORKBOOK

UNIT 6

LESSON 1

1. Look at the pictures and write the sports. Then complete with the verbs related to the sports.

catch   hit   jump   kick   run   throw

tennis

1

hit
jump
run

2
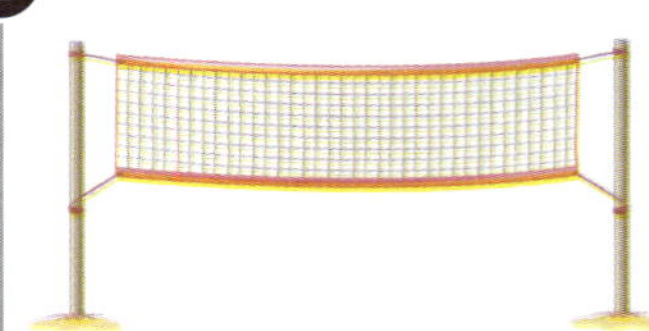

3

4

5
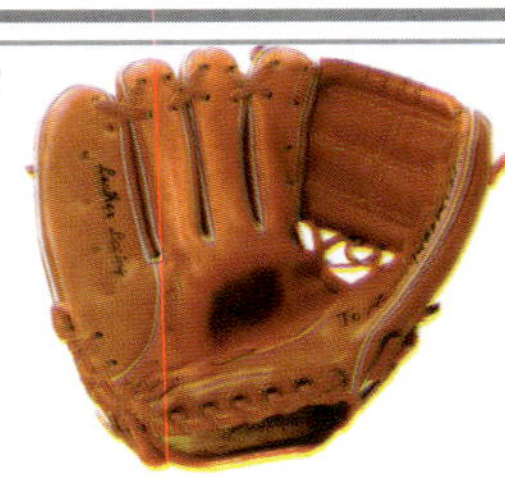

6

LESSON 2

1. Look at the chart. Write *can* or *can't*.

		 Avery	 Grant	 Ricardo and Laura	You
	play baseball	✔	✘	✔	
	play basketball	✘	✘	✘	
	play soccer	✔	✘	✘	
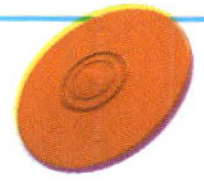	play Ultimate	✔	✘	✔	
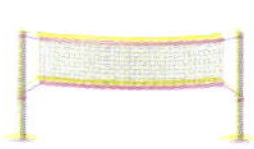	play volleyball	✘	✔	✘	

1. Avery <u>can't</u> play volleyball.
2. Ricardo and Laura _____ play Ultimate.
3. Avery _____ play soccer.
4. Ricardo and Laura _____ play basketball.
5. Grant _____ play baseball.
6. Avery _____ play basketball.

2. Answer the questions.

1. Can Grant play basketball? <u>No, he can't</u>.
2. Can Avery play baseball? ________________.
3. Can Ricardo and Laura play volleyball? ________________.
4. Can Grant play volleyball? ________________.

3. Complete the **you** column of the chart. Write sentences.

LESSON 3

1. Match.

1 

2 

3 

4 

5 

6  a

a. ~~Get enough sleep.~~
b. Don't exercise
c. Drink water.
d. Eat good food.
e. Have fun!
f. Keep clean.

2. Answer the questions.

1. In your opinion, is it important to get enough sleep?
   Yes, it is. / No, it isn't ______________________.
2. Can you keep clean at school?
   ______________________.
3. Is the food at your school good?
   ______________________.
4. Can you drink water at school?
   ______________________.
5. In your opinion, is it important to have fun?
   ______________________.
6. What's your favorite type of exercise?
   ______________________.

LESSON 4

1. What is your opinion of a sports camp? Check ✓.

- ☐ It's really cool!
- ☐ It's interesting, but I'm not good at sports.
- ☐ It's not fun.

2. Read about Pro Sports Camp. Then answer the questions.

PRO SPORTS CAMP

WELCOME TO OUR CAMP! AT PRO SPORTS CAMP, YOU CAN PLAY YOUR SPORT AND PLAY NEW SPORTS TOO!

What's your favorite sport? Come play it at Pro Sports Camp! You can learn with professional coaches! There's soccer, baseball, basketball, and tennis. There's also table tennis, Ultimate, and swimming.

At Pro Sports Camp, you can make new friends, eat good food, exercise, and play your favorite sport. Come to Pro Sports Camp and have fun!

Pro Sports Camp is in beautiful California, and there are twenty-five cabins at our camp. There are two bedrooms per cabin, and there are four beds in each bedroom. There are two bathrooms in the cabin too. There's no wi-fi, and you can't use your cell phone. It's a sports camp, not a technology camp!

1. What is the name of the camp? Pro Sports Camp.
2. Can you play basketball at Pro Sports Camp? ______________________.
3. Can you play handball at the camp? ______________________.
4. How many cabins are there? ______________________.
5. Is there wi-fi at the camp? ______________________.
6. Can you eat good food at the camp? ______________________.

WORKBOOK

UNIT 7

LESSON 1

1. Look at the chart. Then complete the sentences.

in the morning

in the afternoon

in the evening

at night

1. We eat dinner in the evening.
2. We go to bed __________.
3. We eat breakfast __________.
4. We come home __________.

2. Use the words from the box to complete the expressions.

a shower	dinner	up
~~breakfast~~	to bed	to school
homework	lunch	home

eat breakfast / __________ / __________

get __________

do __________

go __________ / __________

come __________

take __________

LESSON 2

1. Look at the chart. Then complete the sentences about the girl using the simple present. Use *don't* in the negative sentences.

eat breakfast with my family	✗	✓
go to school in the morning	✓	✗
eat lunch at school	✓	✗
come home at 3:00 p.m.	✓	✗
do homework in the evening	✗	✓
take a shower in the evening	✓	✗
go to bed at 10:00 p.m.	✓	✓

1. I ___eat___ lunch at school.
2. I ________ homework in the evening.
3. I ________ home at 3:00 p.m.
4. I ________ to bed at 10:00 p.m.
5. I ________ a shower in the evening.
6. I ________ breakfast with my family.

2. Now answer the questions about the boys.

1. Do they do homework in the evening? Yes, they do.
2. Do they eat lunch at school? ____________________
3. Do they go to bed at 10:00 p.m.? ____________________
4. Do they take a shower in the evening? ____________________
5. Do they come home at 3:00 p.m.? ____________________
6. Do they eat breakfast with their families? ____________________

3. Answer the questions about yourself.

1. Do you go to school in the morning? ____________________
2. Do you eat breakfast with your family? ____________________
3. Do you eat lunch at school? ____________________
4. Do you take a shower in the evening? ____________________
5. Do you go to bed at 10:00 p.m.? ____________________

LESSON 3

1. What time is it? Write.

1  It's 5:40.

2  ______

3  ______

4  ______

5  ______

6  ______

2. Write the missing words.

1. What time is it? It's five fifteen.

2. What ______ is it? It's ______.

3. What ______ it? It's ______.

3. Answer the questions.

1. What time do you get up? I get up at 7:30.
2. What time do you eat breakfast? I eat breakfast at ______.
3. What time do you go to school? I go to school at ______.
4. What time do you go to bed? ______.

LESSON 4

1. **Read the first three lines of the interview. Then answer these questions.**

1. What is the band's name? ______________________
2. Who are the singers? ______________________
3. Where are they? ______________________

Melissa: Hi! I'm Melissa Phillips and I'm here in New York with 22 Trees, our favorite band! Hello, Ian, Pete, Danny, Howie, and Zach!
Ian: Hi, Melissa.
Melissa: What time do you get up?
Ian: We get up at one in the afternoon. We do concerts at night.
Melissa: Wow! What time do you go to bed?
Ian: At 4:00 or 5:00 in the morning.
Melissa: Really? And when do you eat breakfast?
Ian: We eat breakfast in the afternoon, and then we do homework. Our teacher is here, on our bus.
Melissa: When do you eat lunch?
Ian: In the evening, at 6:00.
Melissa: Then what?
Ian: Then we practice, or take a shower, or play soccer or basketball.
Melissa: When do you do concerts?
Ian: We sing from 8:00 to 11:00 and then we eat dinner.
Melissa: You eat dinner at 11:00?
Ian: No, we eat dinner at 12:00 or 1:00. Then we play video games and go to bed at 4:00.
Melissa: Wow! Thank you, Ian and the 22 Trees. That's an interesting routine!

2. **Read the interview. Then answer T (true) or F (false).**

1. The singers go to bed at 4:00 or 5:00 in the morning. ☐
2. They do concerts in the morning. ☐
3. Their teacher is on their bus. ☐
4. They eat lunch at 6:00 in the evening. ☐
5. They play soccer or basketball in the morning. ☐
6. They eat dinner at 11:00. ☐

WORKBOOK

UNIT 8

LESSON 1

1. Unscramble the food names.

1. s g e g ______ eggs ______
2. e n s b a ____________
3. t a s k e ____________
4. h s i f ____________
5. a p t a s ____________
6. c e i r a c m e ____________
7. r a e b d ____________
8. c n h i k e c ____________
9. e r c i ____________

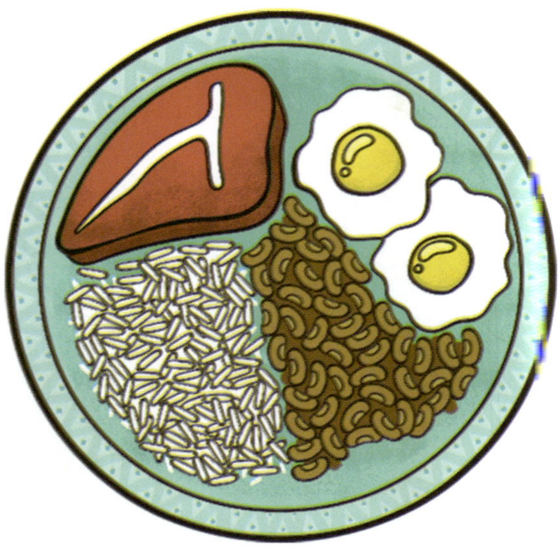

2. When do you eat these food items? Write the words from **Activity 1** in the boxes below.

AT BREAKFAST	AT LUNCH	AT DINNER
____________	____________	____________
____________	____________	____________
____________	____________	____________
____________	____________	____________

3. Number the foods 1 – 9. Write 1 = *My favorite!* to 9 = *I don't like it.*

beans	☐	eggs	☐	pasta	☐
bread	☐	fish	☐	rice	☐
chicken	☐	ice cream	☐	steak	☐

LESSON 2

1. Read about these students and complete the chart with ✗ or ✓.

Fabio likes chicken, steak, salad, and ice cream. He doesn't like rice and beans, and bread.

Juliana likes fish, pasta, bread, and ice cream, but she doesn't like steak, eggs, and salad.

Brenda likes eggs, rice and beans, pasta, and salad, but she doesn't like chicken, fish, and ice cream.

William likes fish, rice and beans, and eggs, but he doesn't like chicken, pasta, bread, and steak.

Fabio	✗	✓							
Juliana									
Brenda									
William									
Family member									

2. Look at the chart again. Write *likes* or *doesn't like*.

1. William likes rice and beans.
2. Juliana __________ eggs.
3. Brenda __________ pasta.
4. Fabio __________ ice cream.
5. William __________ chicken.
6. Brenda __________ fish.

3. Complete the chart about a family member. Then write sentences.

My brother doesn't like eggs.

LESSON 3

1. Circle the words in the word snake.

2. Circle the correct words to form questions and answers.

	1.	Do	he	want	sushi?	Yes,	she	does.
		Does	she	wants		No,	he	doesn't.
	2.	Does	he	want	pizza?	Yes,	she	does.
		Do	she	wants		No,	he	doesn't.
	3.	Do	he	want	tacos?	Yes,	they	does.
		Does	they	wants		No,	he	do.
	4.	Does	they	want	noodles?	Yes,	they	don't.
		Do	she	wants		No,	she	doesn't.
	5.	Does	he	wants	fish and chips?	No,	she	does.
		Do	she	want		Yes,	he	doesn't.
	6.	Do	he	wants	a hamburger?	No,	she	does.
		Does	she	want		Yes,	he	doesn't.

LESSON 4

1. Look at the pictures in **Activity 2**. Check ✔ the things you can see.

pizza	☐	chicken	☐
salad	☐	French fries	☐

2. Read and answer **T** (true) or **F** (false).

www.restaurantfood.com/us

RESTAURANT FOOD IN THE USA

When you travel to the USA, you can eat in lots of types of restaurants.

There are about 232,000 fast food restaurants in the USA. and they're very popular. At American fast food restaurants, you can eat hamburgers and French fries. At fast food restaurants, you can also eat chicken, sandwiches, tacos, pizza, fish, and salad. Fast food restaurants are cheap, but they aren't very healthy. Be careful!

You can eat "fast casual" food too. There are sandwiches, soups, and salads. It's not fast food, but it's not an expensive restaurant.

Ethnic food — food from around the world — is popular too. There are delicious restaurants with food from Mexico, China, Japan, Italy, and Brazil.

There are expensive restaurants too. You can eat steak, pasta, fish, and chicken, and other things. These restaurants can be expensive, but the food is very good!

1. Hamburgers and French fries are cheap at fast food restaurants. T
2. There's salad at fast food restaurants, too. ☐
3. There's cheap pizza at fast casual restaurants. ☐
4. Ethnic food is food from the USA. ☐

VERB LIST

VERB	SIMPLE PAST	PAST PARTICIPLE	TRANSLATION
awake	awoke	awoken	acordar
be	was/were	been	ser; estar
become	became	become	tornar-se
begin	began	begun	começar
break	broke	broken	quebrar; transgredir
bring	brought	brought	trazer
build	built	built	construir
burn	burned	burned	queimar
buy	bought	bought	comprar
catch	caught	caught	pegar; capturar
choose	chose	chosen	escolher
come	came	come	vir; chegar
cost	cost	cost	custar
cut	cut	cut	cortar
do	did	done	fazer; realizar
draw	drew	drawn	desenhar; puxar; atrair
dream	dreamed	dreamed	sonhar
drink	drank	drunk	beber
drive	drove	driven	dirigir; conduzir; impulsionar
eat	ate	eaten	comer
fall	fell	fallen	cair; baixar
feel	felt	felt	sentir
fight	fought	fought	lutar; combater; brigar
find	found	found	achar; encontrar
fly	flew	flown	voar
forget	forgot	forgotten	esquecer(-se)
forgive	forgave	forgiven	perdoar
freeze	froze	frozen	congelar
get	got	got/gotten	conseguir; obter
give	gave	given	dar; ceder
go	went	gone	ir; partir; sumir
grow	grew	grown	crescer
have	had	had	ter

VERB	SIMPLE PAST	PAST PARTICIPLE	TRANSLATION
hear	heard	heard	ouvir
hit	hit	hit	bater; acertar; atingir
hurt	hurt	hurt	machucar; ferir; magoar
know	knew	known	saber; conhecer
learn	learned	learned	aprender; descobrir
leave	left	left	sair; deixar
let	let	let	deixar; permitir
lose	lost	lost	perder
make	made	made	fazer
pay	paid	paid	pagar; prestar
put	put	put	pôr; colocar
quit	quit	quit	largar; desistir
read	read	read	ler
run	ran	run	correr
say	said	said	dizer
see	saw	seen	enxergar; ver
sell	sold	sold	vender
send	sent	sent	enviar
sing	sang	sung	cantar
sit	sat	sat	sentar(-se)
sleep	slept	slept	dormir
speak	spoke	spoken	falar
swim	swam	swum	nadar
take	took	taken	levar; tirar; pegar; receber
teach	taught	taught	ensinar
tell	told	told	contar; dizer
think	thought	thought	pensar; achar
throw	threw	thrown	lançar; atirar; arremessar; jogar
understand	understood	understood	entender
wake	woke	woken	acordar
wear	wore	worn	vestir; usar
win	won	won	vencer
write	wrote	written	escrever